General editor: Graham Handley MA Ph.D.

Brodie's Notes on Alice Walker's
The Color Purple

Marian Picton BA Ph.D.
Head of English, Hugh Baird College, Bootle

Pan Books London, Sydney and Auckland

First published 1991 by
Pan Books Ltd, Cavaye Place, London SW10 9PG

9 8 7 6 5 4 3 2 1

© Pan Books Ltd 1991

ISBN 0 330 50328 6

Photoset by Parker Typesetting Service, Leicester

Printed in England by Clays Ltd, St Ives plc

Contents

Page references in these Notes are to the Women's Press edition of *The Color Purple*, but references are also given to the individual letters, so that the Notes may be used with any edition of the novel.

The author and publisher wish to thank Alice Walker, and The Women's Press, for permission to reproduce extracts from *The Color Purple*, and from Alice Walker's two volumes of poetry, *Horses Make a Landscape Look More Beautiful* and *Good Night, Willie Lee, I'll See You in the Morning*.

Preface by the general editor

The intention throughout this study aid is to stimulate and guide, to encourage your involvement in the book, and to develop informed responses and a sure understanding of the main details.

Brodie's Notes provide a clear outline of the play or novel's plot, followed by act, scene, or chapter summaries and/or commentaries. These are designed to emphasize the most important literary and factual details. Poems, stories or non-fiction texts combine brief summary with critical commentary on individual aspects or common features of the genre being examined. Textual notes define what is difficult or obscure and emphasize literary qualities. Revision questions are set at appropriate points to test your ability to appreciate the prescribed book and to write accurately and relevantly about it.

In addition, each of these Notes includes a critical appreciation of the author's art. This covers such major elements as characterization, style, structure, setting and themes. Poems are examined technically – rhyme, rhythm, for instance. In fact, any important aspect of the prescribed work will be evaluated. The aim is to send you back to the text you are studying.

Each study aid concludes with a series of general questions which require a detailed knowledge of the book: some of these questions may invite comparison with other books, some will be suitable for coursework exercises, and some could be adapted to work you are doing on another book or books. Each study aid has been adapted to meet the needs of the current examination requirements. They provide a basic, individual and imaginative response to the work being studied, and it is hoped that they will stimulate you to acquire disciplined reading habits and critical fluency.

Graham Handley 1991

Alice Walker's life and work

Alice Walker is a black feminist. All her work is dominated by these two interests, though the range of that work is wide, including lecturing and editing as well as writing four volumes of poetry, miscellaneous essays and articles and several full-length novels. Some of her writing is autobiographical, more of it highly personal; almost all of it has a certain propagandist element, a deep compassion for the way in which blacks and women, and particularly black women, have been treated, and a faith that when these evils have been revealed they can be improved.

She was born in 1944 in Eatonton, Georgia, and the influence of her upbringing in the Deep South, with its legacy of racial oppression, is clearly to be seen in her work. *The Temple of My Familiar*, as well as some shorter pieces, draws on the memory of slavery. More important than slavery itself in Ms Walker's work, however, is the period in which the blacks were nominally free but subject to all kinds of oppression through racial hatred and the exploitation of their labour; when in fact the protection of slavery had been removed without giving social or economic opportunity in its place. The slave owner had at least some incentive to look after his property, but the white employer cannot be held accountable for the poverty and misery in which his black workers live. If they become successful, he may be envious or feel threatened and react violently. At best he has had a long tradition of thinking blacks to be naturally inferior. This is the background to much incidental detail in *The Color Purple*, particularly in the treatment of Sofia, while the fight for deseg-regation and voting rights that was the object of the Civil Rights movements of the sixties, and in which Ms Walker took an active part, forms the subject of *Meridian*. Georgia is present in many of her works not merely as a landscape of cows and cotton fields, but as a deep anger against the plight of the rural poor.

In her twenties, she had for the first time the opportunity to make trips to Uganda and Kenya, and this again has become a major influence in her work. As with so many black Americans, she has a sense of involvement with Africa, and the possibility of tracing back elements of black culture to African roots forms an important element in *The Temple of My Familiar*. This is not involvement which is limited to folk history, however, nor is it uncritical. She acknowledges a debt to certain African writers, and shares their concern for the political and cultural problems of their societies. In particular there are thematic resemblances between the novel of Ngugi wa Thiong'o, *Petals of Blood*, and the episodes with the Olinka in *The Color Purple*, concerning the economic exploitation of Africans and the disintegration of their tribal culture. She adds to this her own dominant concern, however, for the women of Africa, undervalued, under-educated, and exploited by patriarchal systems.

For it is always the condition of women which is her primary concern. Even in a novel like *The Third Life of Grange Copeland*, nominally about Grange and his son Brownfield, it is the women who are the real focus of attention. Many of her stories were first published in the feminist periodical *Ms*, of which she is a consulting editor. She calls herself, however, not 'feminist' but 'womanist', a word coined to indicate a profound faith in the capabilities of black women, and has commented on one occasion that 'womanist is to feminist as purple is to lavender': the commitment is as profound as that. Besides the tendency for the women in her work to be the strong characters, and the men often brutal or violent out of ignorance or weakness, she has many of the classic feminist preoccupations. Her work contains a number of different treatments of the problem of rape – there are two, after all, in *The Color Purple* alone, plus a failed attempt on Nettie. There are also powerful condemnations of pornography involving the exploitation of women. In *The Temple of My Familiar*, for instance, Suwelo, the man who has married Celie's granddaughter (for the story of *The Color Purple* partly continues into this novel) comments as he reads a trashy novel that his generation has failed women and themselves. Ms Walker's essay 'Coming Apart', published in *You Can't Keep a Good Woman Down*, has some interesting insights into the problem. This essay itself was 'labelled pornographic', she says, and her work as a whole contains more sexual violence than might be to some people's taste; but its object is certainly not titillation. She writes, 'I believe it is only by writing stories in which pornography is confronted openly and explicitly that writers can make a contribution, in their own medium, to a necessary fight.'

It is probably the four volumes of poetry she has so far

published which give the greatest insights into what Alice Walker herself is like, for the style is simple and direct and the subjects personal. She writes, for instance, about the preparations for a visit from her daughter, Rebecca; while the Willie Lee of *Good Night, Willie Lee, I'll See You in the Morning* is her father. There are love poems; poems which reflect her knowledge of Africa; comments on racial violence; tributes to other women. Whatever the subject, these verses have a feeling of directness and honesty about them, clear and balanced, as in:

These days I think of Rebecca
'Mama, are you a racist?' she asks.
And I realize I have badmouthed white people
once too often
in her presence.

The style of her poetry is poignant and straightforward, employing short lines and indulging only sparingly in the tricks of rhetoric. She is careful how the words are placed on the page and in that way has a tight control over the rhythms, but apparently has little liking for the artifice of metre. In fact her verse often contains a suggestion of the reflective speaking voice:

the fundamental question about revolution
as lorraine hansberry was not afraid to know
is not simply whether i am willing to give up my life
but if i am prepared to give up my comfort.

This talent for emotive simplicity, and ear for the rhythms of speech, is particularly suitable for the creation of naïve characters like Celie, whose style in *The Color Purple*, with its short, emphatic and economical sentences, is much livelier than Nettie's more involved syntax, and it seems likely that Alice Walker's experience as a poet has made a major contribution to the success of that novel.

One final quality which must be mentioned is the sense of humour, the wit, which emerges from these poems. When the appropriate reaction to so much that she has to write about is pity and anger it might be possible to overlook this, but the face that looks out from the photographs on the covers of Alice Walker's books is a shrewdly humorous as well as an attractive one and this, too, is reflected in her verse – as, for instance, in the poem 'Every Morning':

'Don't you see that person
staring at you?' I ask my breasts,
which are still capable
of staring back.
'If I didn't exercise
you couldn't look up
that far.
Your life would be nothing
but shoes.'

And perhaps here a comment which is made in *The Temple of My Familiar* by Celie's daughter, Olivia, is relevant. She says of Celie's speech that it had 'a perkiness, a plainness, that was sometimes humorous but always compelling'. Celie of course is deliberately uneducated and inarticulate – 'a literal speaker' – the circumstances of her life necessarily make her so. But it is possible that what makes Celie easily Alice Walker's most successful and original character to date is the fact that Ms Walker, on a far, far more sophisticated level, has these qualities too.

A note on the film of *The Color Purple* by Steven Spielberg

Some students may well approach *The Color Purple* for the first time through the medium of film or video, and it is important to be aware of the differences between the two versions of the work. Spielberg's version of the novel contains some excellent acting and some memorable images, such as the moment when Celie is sharpening the razor with a desire to cut Albert's throat; the film cuts to and fro between that and the knife being prepared for the scarification of Adam and Tashi in order to build up tension and a sense of violence. In general, however, the film version has been considerably sentimentalized.

This is most noticeable in the presentation of Celie herself, who is depicted in the novel as a brutalized drudge, accustomed to hard agricultural labour. The film, however, begins with an image of Celie and Nettie frisking happily through fields of flowers, the rape which occurs on page one of the novel being very lightly skated over – understandably in a film which has a '15' certificate. As the wife of Mr—, Celie certainly has to cope with domestic problems, but she does so wearing a series of very fetching outfits, usually with earrings, whereas the Celie of the novel owes her first suitable dress to the intervention of Mr—'s sister, who points out her rags. Her conversion to wearing trousers, powerful symbol of emancipation in the original, is almost entirely omitted; she makes a pair for Harpo, who looks faintly ridiculous in them; and Celie in the film takes over her inheritance wearing a tight skirt and high heels.

Similarly, the major images of Africa, which in the novel explore the degrading effects of the destruction of the Olinka religion and economy together, become fantasies of giraffe, zebra and elephants in Celie's imagination, with some rather pretty pictures of a game reserve interspersed with those of the road which destroys the Olinka village. It is only fair to say, however, that one of the sharpest comments on the African life – Olivia's comments that the African men are 'like white people at home who don't want colored people to learn' – is clearly made.

All films of novels have to make alterations, and usually film makers are compelled to simplify the plot a little because the running time of a film is obviously so much shorter than the reading time of a novel. Casualties in the plot line here include the lesbian relationship of Celie and Shug, represented by one kiss, and the role of Mary Agnes. Although Mary Agnes does figure in the film, her importance is reduced, and her sacrifice in order to help Sofia, in which she is raped by her uncle, is omitted. Originally, Mary Agnes had a much greater contribution to make on the theme of the sisterhood of women and their need for independence, but these feminist elements in the novel have been diminished.

Spielberg conveys well the comic elements in the character of Sofia and her relationship with Harpo, although again the relationship has necessarily been somewhat simplified; his Sofia throws some formidable punches. Visually memorable is the way Shug's explanation of her religion takes place in a field of purple flowers, the slight sentimentality here being entirely appropriate, and then the way Nettie reappears from Africa with a purple cloth round her shoulders. Spielberg also conveys economically the bond of love between Celie and Nettie, using a little childhood clapping game to do so, which is simple and effective. He is much better, however, on the sisters than on the 'sisterhood'. A film of *The Color Purple* which substantially evades the love of Celie and Shug, and 'fudges' the major feminist issues, must be treated with some caution as a representation of the novel or a commentary on it.

Synopsis

The fourteen-year-old Celie has been raped by Alphonso, her mother's husband, whom she believes to be her father. She writes about her experiences to God because she has no one else to turn to; the only person she has to love is her younger sister, Nettie. She bears Alphonso two children, both of whom are taken from her and given away. Her mother dies before the second child is born.

She is married off before she is twenty to Albert, whom she knows as Mr—, and brings up his four children. Celie's sister, Nettie, lives with her for a time, but is forced to leave when Mr— wants to make love to her. In revenge, because she rejects his advances, Mr— withholds Nettie's letters to her sister, and it is some time before she is heard of again. Celie's marriage is a very unhappy one. Mr— really loves Shug Avery, a singer who has had three children by him: he treats Celie as a domestic drudge and beats her.

M—'s children grow up and leave, except the eldest boy, Harpo. He wants to marry Sofia, who is expecting his baby, but his father disapproves, and it is some time before Harpo finds the courage to assert himself. When he does marry, although he loves her he cannot accept that Sofia, who is a very strong-minded woman, is his equal. He tries to beat her into submission, but fails. The marriage lasts some time, because they have five children, but eventually Sofia leaves, and her sixth child is another man's.

Meanwhile Shug Avery becomes very ill while singing in the town. Albert takes her home and Celie nurses her back to health. A friendship develops between Celie and Shug. Six months after Sofia leaves him, Harpo makes his home into a jukejoint and Shug, now recovering from her illness, sings at it. She dedicates a song to Celie.

One night at the jukejoint Sofia returns. She has a fight with Harpo's new girlfriend, Mary Agnes, and knocks two of her teeth out. Soon after, Sofia gets into a quarrel with the wife of the mayor of the town, by refusing to be her maid. She is badly beaten up and sentenced to twelve years in prison. Mary Agnes helps to get her transferred from the prison to be the mayor's maid after all, but this is the most her friends can do for her. Life returns to normal: Shug goes away to renew her singing career; Mary Agnes becomes a singer herself; Sofia seethes with resentment, but adapts to life as a maid.

Five years pass, then Shug arrives at Albert's home on a visit. To everyone's surprise she is married, to a man named Grady. Albert and Celie are both extremely jealous. One night when the men have gone out together, Shug comes into Celie's bed, and Celie tells her about her early life with Alphonso. Shug kisses her in sympathy at first, then makes love to her physically.

Shug also finds out about Celie's affection for Nettie, and how she never hears from her sister. She discovers that Nettie has actually been writing for years, but that Albert has been concealing the letters. The women find where the packet of letters is hidden and secretly read them.

It turns out that, on leaving Celie, Nettie went to live with a preacher called Samuel and his wife, Corinne, who had unknowingly adopted Celie's children. These two wish to become missionaries in Africa, and take Nettie there with them. Even though she never receives any reply to her letters, Nettie continues to write over the years because she is so lonely. On discovering how Albert has behaved over this, Celie wants to kill him, and is only restrained by Shug.

In Africa, Nettie has settled among the Olinka tribe, and works as a missionary, teaching and nursing. She writes in detail about the Olinka way of life and customs, especially the way in which the women are treated. After a few years, a road is constructed through the Olinka settlement, and this destroys the community. Corinne also becomes jealous of Nettie and worried because the children resemble her, imagining that Nettie and her husband have had an affair. Samuel reveals to Nettie that he knows some details of her early life and Celie's, the most important of which is that Alphonso was not their father, and so the children are not the result of incest. On discovering this, Celie is overwhelmed.

Nettie's letters continue with the death of Corinne. Now that she knows her sister is alive, Celie addresses her letters to Nettie instead of God. She writes about the way she has rejected her old view of religion, because her image of God was that of a man. Shug, however, has convinced her that God does exist, although in a different form, and that it can be worshipped through love and joy.

Celie decides to leave Albert and go away to Memphis, where Shug has a house. Mary Agnes also decides to leave Harpo, in order to become a professional singer. Sofia has been released, after eleven and a half years, and has returned home, so she looks after Mary Agnes' child by Harpo as well as her own. Albert is scathing about Celie's decision, and as she leaves with Shug she curses him bitterly. Grady goes off with Mary Agnes.

In Memphis Celie starts a new life. While Shug is working, Celie begins to make trousers, and these are so successful that her occupation turns into a profitable business. When she goes back to visit Harpo and Sofia she finds that Albert had a breakdown after she left but was helped by Harpo and is now a reformed character. He began to recover when Harpo made him send Celie the rest of Nettie's letters.

Nettie now describes how the Olinka people have been deprived of their land and their culture destroyed. She has tried to get help from England but failed. She is also now married to Samuel. Celie's son, Adam, is in love with an Olinka girl called Tashi and deeply distressed because Tashi has allowed the tribe to put ritual scars on her face. Life with the Olinka is becoming unbearable, and Nettie's family are thinking of coming home.

Alphonso dies and Celie inherits considerable property from her parents, which he had kept from her, including a fine house. Her happiness is spoiled, however, when Shug has an affair with a young man called Germaine who plays the flute in her band. Celie is bitterly jealous. She is also worried because Sofia's youngest child, Henrietta, is ill with a blood disorder which can only be controlled by a diet of yams, a food which the child detests and refuses to eat. Then a telegram arrives to say that the ship on which Nettie was returning from Africa has been sunk by German mines (the action now taking place during the Second World War).

Letters from Nettie continue to arrive, however. Sofia quarrels about race relations with Eleanor Jane, the mayor's daughter, but afterwards makes it up when Eleanor Jane understands her position and is really helpful in caring for Henrietta. Celie's relations with Albert improve and they become friends. Finally Shug separates from Germaine and returns to Celie. The very last letter completes the happy ending, when Nettie and Samuel unexpectedly arrive at Celie's house and she is reunited with them, her children, and her son's wife, Tashi.

Letter summaries, critical commentary and textual notes

The letters have been numbered here for convenience, but they are not so in the published text. Page references are to the Women's Press paperback edition, 1983, but obviously they follow the chronological order of any other edition.

Letter 1 (p. 3)

The epigraph, 'You better not never tell nobody but God. It'd kill your mammy,' explains the rather unusual form of the book. There are plenty of other novels written in the form of letters or diaries, but they usually have a human audience. Celie, however, is entirely alone, cut off from other people not only by the circumstances of her life but also by the guilty nature of her secret. She thinks that the man who has raped her and made her pregnant is her father, and it is only years later that she discovers he was her stepfather.

The date is the beginning of the twentieth century, and Celie at this time is still a child of fourteen. Her childishness and ignorance of the world show in every line, in the short, clipped sentences and elementary vocabulary, for she is uneducated as well as very young. From the beginning she appears as a totally innocent victim. She is bewildered more than anything by what is happening to her. The way she crosses out 'I am' and substitutes 'have always been' a good girl is pathetic; it implies that, childlike, she feels that what has happened is in some way her own responsibility, whereas a more experienced person would have been simply outraged. The naïve and literal way in which she describes the sexual experience is also pathetic, and we feel for her physical suffering as well as her mental shock.

The plain, superficially very simple, style of these early letters is carefully calculated by the author. The style itself builds up the portrait of Celie while she tells us of her background. What has happened is plainly obvious to the reader from the deadpan way in which Celie reports it, even though she herself does not understand. Her mother, who is in poor health, has refused to have sexual intercourse with her husband immediately after the birth of her baby because she is too weak. The husband, briefly left alone with Celie and the other children, has brutally used her instead to satisfy his lust. It makes a remarkably dramatic opening to the novel.

fussing Quarrelling.
Fonso Alphonso.

Letter 2 (p. 4)

Considerable time often elapses between letters. About eighteen months must have passed now, because Celie has been delivered of the first child, Olivia, and is now heavily pregnant with the second, Adam. Her sexual ignorance and the appalling neglect with which she has been treated are emphasized by her description of her first baby's birth, which came as a complete surprise to her. The circumstances of her life, bad enough before, have now worsened, because her baby has been taken from her without explanation and she thinks it may have been murdered: her mother is dead, having cursed Celie rather than comforting her. It is also apparent that Celie is having to do very heavy domestic work in spite of her condition. These are two themes which are important in the novel – the way women are exploited as household drudges, and the real hardship of caring for numbers of children in primitive conditions.

Letter 3 (p. 5)

This letter is written immediately after the birth of Celie's second baby, and at least introduces a ray of hope that the child may be alive, even though this one as well has been callously removed, leaving her grieving. Alphonso's character has not improved, however, as he is now looking lustfully at Nettie. We see Celie's love for her younger sister in her determination to protect her. Another aspect of the persecution of Celie, and an important feminist theme, appears for the first time: while persecuted, she is criticized for not looking attractive. Few men behave well in this novel.

Letter 4 (p. 6)

Alphonso has now married a girl of about sixteen: he seems to have a taste for very young girls. This letter illustrates not only how girls are sexually exploited by men, 'He be on her all the time,' but also another aspect of their harsh lives, the difficulty of looking after large numbers of children. Alice Walker never underestimates the labour which this involves, and the exhaustion. We have in this letter the first mention of Mr— (Albert), who appears as a suitor for Nettie. There is an implied similarity between Alphonso and Albert, even though Albert has 'only' three children. Another disturbing feature of this letter is the background of violence, accepted without comment, simply as fact. Albert's wife was 'kilt by her boyfriend coming home from church'.

kilt Killed.
more then a notion Very hard work.

Letter 5 (p. 7)

More violence occurs, with Celie beaten for supposedly winking at a boy in church. This leads to an important clue to her character and attitudes: she says that she looks only at women 'cause I'm not scared of them'. It takes her most of the next thirty years to overcome the fear of men which is instilled into her in early life by her experiences of lust and violence. At this point, however, Celie somewhat mysteriously becomes infertile, which at least saves her from the oppression of constant childbearing.

big The term Celie nearly always uses for pregnant.

Letter 6 (p. 8)

The importance of this letter is the mention of Shug Avery, the scandalous connection between her and Mr— being one of the reasons why Mr— is not allowed to marry Nettie. Most of the space, however, is given to the effect Shug's photograph has on Celie, who considers her 'the most beautiful woman I ever saw', and begs the picture for herself. Shug is, of course, highly glamorous, but right from the beginning there is also a hint of greater depth to the character in Celie's comment, 'Her eyes serious tho. Sad some.' We are aware how strongly she attracts Celie long before the two actually meet.

like somethin tail Like animal fur.

Letter 7 (p. 9)

We see the extent of Celie's heroic self-sacrifice for those she loves when she deliberately offers her body to Alphonso in order to save Nettie. She is pitiful in the extreme as she tries to dress herself up attractively and only gets a beating in addition to the sexual abuse. This is the letter where Celie's marriage to Mr— is first mentioned, and she is spared no humiliation. Alphonso explains brutally 'She ain't fresh' (i.e. a virgin), without of course mentioning that he himself is the father of her children, entirely against her will. He also describes her as ugly. She is regarded, in fact, as a piece of property. The cow that is offered with her appears to be as important a part of the bargain as Celie herself. Her virtues in the men's eyes are that she can be treated any way they want and exploited, as 'she can work like a man'.

horsehair i.e. used as a hairpiece.
trampy Provocatively.
crib Place for storing animal feed.

Letter 8 (p. 11)

It has already been mentioned that Celie is not considered clever. Here we find one of the reasons why she is uneducated. While she desperately wanted to learn, she was taken away from school at the first signs of pregnancy; and although she has tried since to learn from Nettie, seeing education as a possible means of escape, she has had too many other problems. It is yet another aspect of the trap she is in. Mr—, after a long hesitation, now decides to marry her because he cannot himself cope with his children. Before making the decision he inspects her exactly as if she were a farm animal. The description of the incident, with Mr— not even getting down from his horse and Alphonso reading the paper, makes clear the contempt with which the men regard her. Celie is willing to accept the situation as she thinks this may lead to some means of escape for herself and Nettie. But in any case she is clearly helpless to resist.

the Neater, the Peter, and the Santomareater The ships in which Columbus sailed to America in 1492 were actually called Nina, Pinta and Santa Maria.

Letter 9 (p. 13)

As early as the wedding day, it is clear that Celie's new home is no better than her old; every detail is of some kind of hardship. There are four children, not three as she thought, all badly neglected. The eldest boy injures her. The household work is heavy. In spite of all this we see Celie's courage and generosity as she immediately tackles the problems and even puts her arm around Mr— in bed.

Letter 10 (p. 14)

Celie is now about twenty. The letters begin to lengthen and to show a greater depth of understanding of her surroundings, giving more detail of the incidents and characters with whom she comes into contact; though it is still left to the reader to interpret and react to what is set down mainly as a matter of fact. It is significant that she gives a good deal of attention here to her meeting, in a shop, with the woman we later identify as Corinne, who it turns out has adopted Celie's daughter Olivia. Celie's extreme joy at this encounter emphasizes the deep importance of her attachment to her children. Throughout the novel she is looking for someone to love. It is stretching credibility a little to think that Celie can identify Olivia immediately after six years, but this is explained by the strong physical resemblance between her and Celie which is stressed throughout the novel. The attitude of the shopman who serves Corinne here is significant as an example of the contempt with which whites treat blacks.

daidies Nappies.

Letter 11 (p. 17)

Although Celie is briefly comforted when her sister Nettie runs away from home and comes to live with her, Mr—'s sexual morality is no better than Alphonso's, and as Nettie rejects his advances, he throws her out. This letter is significant in several ways. One is that Nettie correctly identifies the root of Celie's problem with her husband – her inability to stand up to him – but Celie says 'I don't know how to fight. All I know how to do is stay alive.' Another is that it is this letter which establishes the correspondence between the sisters; when asked to write, Nettie says, 'Nothing but death can keep me from it.' Although it is some years before the letters reach Celie she keeps her promise, and so this not only demonstrates the love and loyalty between the sisters but also lays the foundation for all the descriptions of Africa which Alice Walker wishes to introduce later in the book.

to make miration over i.e. that he finds to admire.

Letter 12 (p. 19)

The visit of two of Mr—'s sisters provides a little well-earned praise for Celie and the way she is coping with the household, keeping it clean and caring for the children better than his first wife ever did. Celie is undervalued not only by the men but by herself, so it is important that we realize that she actually is competent, although downtrodden. It is noticeable that both praise and some rudimentary attempts at help come from the women, particularly Kate, who gets Celie some clothes for the first time and tries to make Harpo, Mr—'s eldest son, behave more acceptably. Harpo's response, 'Women work. I'm a man,' followed by Kate's being asked to leave, shows how men have the absolute power in this environment.

Shug Avery is mentioned again, as a disreputable element in Mr—'s past, because he neglected his wife and children to run after her, and we notice how Celie already has an admiration for her that amounts to obsession. Thinking of what colour she would like for her new dress, Celie asks for purple, because she associates it with Shug whom she sees as like a queen. This is the first mention of purple in the novel, and its connection with Shug is immediately significant, as is the fact that it symbolizes not only beauty but power, being a strong and regal colour. Celie ends up, of course, with a dress in a much quieter blue.

direar, newmonya i.e. diarrhoea and pneumonia, of course. Celie
  spells medical words phonetically.
cut his eye at Exchanged glances with.

Letter 13 (p. 22)

Celie has now been married some five years (Harpo is seventeen now) and has been regularly beaten all that time just as an assertion of Mr—'s power over her. When Harpo asks why it happens, he is told, "Cause she my wife.' Harpo himself now wishes to marry, and the implication is that he, too, will expect to beat his wife. Harpo is not even particularly bad-natured. It is just customary in this society for men to show aggression.

Letter 14 (p. 24)

In the next three letters we are prepared for the actual appearance of Shug Avery, first by the news that she is coming to town to sing. Alice Walker creates suspense as Mr—'s preparations show a state of wild excitement and desperate anxiety about his appearance, while Celie is consumed by a desire just to look at Shug.

pomade Hair oil.
hanskers Handkerchiefs.
hick Ignorant countryman.

Letter 15 (p. 26)

This is a continuation of the previous letter, three days later, with Mr— returning from seeing Shug in a state of physical and emotional exhaustion. Celie has been left at home, characteristically doing hard manual labour in the field, but is actually no less excited: 'Questions be running back and forth through my mind,' she says. 'Feel like snakes.' The similarity in their reactions is actually preparing us for their agreement at the end of the novel, although we may not at this stage realize it.

chopping cotton Thinning young plants, and clearing the drill of grass and weeds with a hoe.

Letter 16 (p. 27)

Again, Mr— is in an abnormal emotional state, sitting around all day, looking at nothing. At this point Alice Walker begins to develop an interest that has been briefly mentioned before; the life of Harpo, who now starts to become a more sympathetic figure instead of just one of Celie's burdens. A parallel is drawn between Celie and Harpo, who is 'strong in body but weak in will', and who works beside Celie in the field, equally exploited by his callous and indolent father. The love story of Harpo and

Sofia is also sustained through the next few letters, deferring the actual appearance of Shug and creating further suspense.

Letter 17 (p. 28)

Some of Harpo's family background is filled in here. Both the young people's parents are unsympathetic to their perfectly reasonable love for one another. Sofia's father objects to Harpo because his mother was violently murdered by her lover. (Harpo has nightmares about this; she died in his arms.) Harpo's father objects to Sofia, and is crudely insulting towards her, because she is heavily pregnant (a piece of hypocrisy if ever there was one when he has three illegitimate children by Shug Avery). Interestingly, Sofia is quite equal to the situation. She is a 'big, strong, healthy' girl who always takes the lead in the relationship, and demonstrates that women do not have to be downtrodden. Sofia stands for the inner strength of women throughout the novel. While apparently a little disappointed at Harpo's show of weakness, she is completely undaunted and tells him, 'When you free, me and the baby be waiting.' Significantly, she has a sister who is also strong and who will help her.

chifferobe Chest of drawers and wardrobe combined.
bright skin i.e. pale brown. There is always acute consciousness of shades of skin colour in Alice Walker's novels.

Letter 18 (p. 32)

There is a sufficient time gap since the previous letter for Sofia's baby to have been born. Harpo has eventually found the courage to defy his father, go on strike as far as the farm work is concerned, and marry Sofia. The marriage seems to be working: Harpo is being paid wages and has a tiny house of his own as a result, so independence and spirit are rewarded and Sofia has effectively triumphed over Mr—.

There is frequently an element of comedy associated with Harpo and Sofia, which emerges in the details of their way of life. Here Sofia's baby cries all through the wedding service and 'his mama stop everything to nurse him'.

goose his interest i.e. arouse some enthusiasm.
switch the traces on you Cheat on you.

Letter 19 (p. 34)

Three more years have passed and the marriage of Harpo and Sofia is actually a happy one. The two are complementary as characters if Harpo will only see it. But Harpo is so used to the idea that women should be subservient that he cannot accept Sofia's independent behaviour and asks his father for advice on how to make her do as he says. 'You ever hit her?' his father asks, this being traditional. Surprisingly, Celie gives the same advice, out of jealousy and indignation that Sofia sometimes seems to pity her for her own beatings. Harpo does as they suggest, or at least so we infer, because the next time he appears he is a mass of bruises and has a comically suspicious story about some difficulties with the mule and how he walked into a door. Harpo may be stuck in conventional attitudes, but Sofia is progressing towards liberation.

mind i.e. do as she is told.

Letter 20 (p. 36)

Harpo has evidently not given up, because in the next letter Celie has actually seen them fighting 'like two mens'. One of the points about Sofia is that physically she is quite equal to this, and apparently she wins again as the whole family then goes off for the weekend to see her sister. Again a comic touch is added by the children making mud pies by the creek, totally unconcerned about the wreckage – which indeed does not threaten their security in any way, as Sofia remains an excellent mother throughout. This is important: Sofia is not a failure as a wife. It is just that her abilities and tastes demand independent recognition.

hants Apparitions.

Letter 21 (p. 37)

Celie is sleepless with guilt over her part in these family troubles, one of the very few times Celie is guilty of anything but putting up with too much from other people. The slight fault actually humanizes the character and makes her more credible. In this letter Sofia confronts Celie and they resolve their differences, as the attitude of each is brought into the open. Sofia says, 'I loves Harpo . . . But I'll kill him dead before I let him beat me.' Celie says, 'I ain't never struck a living thing.' Her only consolations seem resignation and duty, expecting a reward in heaven. Sofia's attitude is much more practical: 'You ought to bash Mr— head open, she say. Think about heaven later.' So the quarrel ends in laughter. It also ends with the women making a quilt. Quilts are a frequent symbol in Alice Walker's work, both of co-operation and unity, and of continuity with the past because they are made out of scraps of old fabric.

This conversation brings in a fair amount of background material about the families of the two women. Both their mothers have not only had to cope with the overwork brought about by large numbers of children, but have also needed to defend the children against an overbearing father – without success, because they were themselves cowed. This is regarded as typical of women's lot in life. It is not just Harpo that Sofia is fighting against, but a harsh, male-dominated society where the stronger feel free to abuse the weaker without restraint.

Old Maker i.e. God.

Revision questions

1 Celie is very young at the beginning of the novel. How does this affect our reactions to what happens to her?

2 Discuss the relationship of Celie and Nettie as it is reflected in the early letters. How does Alice Walker distinguish between the two characters?

3 How far are we meant to see women as victims of society in the early letters?

4 Comment on the young Celie's use of language and what this contributes to our understanding of her character.

Letter 22 (p. 40)

Shug Avery appears at last, in a suitably dramatic fashion, very ill and rejected by the whole community except Mr— and Celie, who both react with extreme emotion. Celie becomes desperately self-conscious about her appearance, just like Mr—

when he went to hear Shug sing earlier, but realizes she can do nothing to make herself attractive. Shug 'look like she ain't long for this world but dressed well for the next', glamorous even while sick, and very bad tempered. Her first words to Celie are spiteful: 'You sure *is* ugly,' she says. It is part of Shug's vitality that she can be harsh and demanding; there is actually not much that is sugary about her in spite of her name. Her behaviour here acts as a contrast to her later kindness.

two berkulosis i.e. tuberculosis, another of Celie's medical misspellings.

Letter 23 (p. 43)

Mr— is now referred to by his proper name of Albert, as he becomes more sharply individualized, although Celie does not realize momentarily that it is his name, a measure of the distance between them. No longer merely the overbearing male, he is humanized by his love for Shug. In fact, he shows weakness in this situation (whereas it brings out Celie's inner strength) and, ill as she is, Shug bullies him and orders him about. When she looks at him Celie notices now that he has a weak chin. It is also the first time that Celie and her husband have ever admitted having an interest in common.

Letter 24 (p. 45)

The relationship between Celie and Shug starts to deepen, as Celie nurses Shug. She is delighted by the sight of Shug's naked body in the bath and says, 'I thought I had turned into a man.' Alice Walker stresses the intimacy of the scene as a prelude to the later love between the women. At the same time Celie is overawed by Shug and calls her respectfully 'ma'am' until told to stop. Although hostile at first, the two women start to exchange a little personal information. They talk about their children, not as yet in any detail, but, as each has been separated from them, there is just a little common ground even at this stage.

her mouth just pack with claws i.e. she makes catty remarks.

Letter 25 (p. 46)

Caring for an invalid happens to be just the kind of situation that shows Celie at her best; it brings out all her kindness, thought for others, and her practical ingenuity. She is portrayed as a character who would care for anyone who needed it, being good, for instance, even to Mr—'s difficult children. But she has had a virtually obsessive interest in Shug from the time she first heard of her, and is now very moved by Shug's closeness, badly wanting to touch her. She does not argue with Shug, who is rejecting food, but eats particularly tempting things like home-cured ham in front of her. It works, for Celie, although uneducated, is shrewd in all practical things. Mr—, meanwhile, has been almost 'crazy' with anxiety. His overwhelming love for Shug, as well as Celie's, contributes to making Shug such a dominant character. We partly accept his evaluation of her.

grits Coarse oatmeal which is made into a kind of porridge.
flapjacks Pancakes.
biscuits What the British call 'scones'.

Letter 26 (p. 48)

Yet another intimate scene between the women follows, with Celie combing Shug's hair while Shug makes up a song. This is the point where Shug starts to affect Celie's values and judgement of life. She says of the tune, 'Sound low down dirty to me. Like what the preacher tell you its sin to hear.' It is the beginning of Celie's real education. In the end it is Shug who becomes her 'preacher' as well as teaching her that sexual love is not 'dirty' but joyful. Shug also makes up a song connected with Celie, presumably the one she sings in letter 33 'about some no count man doing her wrong'.

Letter 27 (p. 49)

Another disagreeable parent, Mr—'s father, appears, to complain about the appearance of Shug in his son's house and generally revile her. Few of the parents in this novel who are allowed to keep their children have satisfactory relations with them. Ironically those who have love to offer, like Celie or Sofia, spend much time separated from theirs. Celie expresses her opinion of Mr—'s father in a memorable gesture, by quietly spitting into his glass of water. Meeting her husband's eyes as his father leaves she realizes that 'this the closest us ever felt,' – an unconventional development of a marriage relationship, but one which is entirely plausible within the terms of the novel.

This visit is closely followed by another from Mr—'s brother, Tobias, another disagreeable character, but one who this time is an admirer of Shug and arrives bearing a box of chocolates. He interrupts a peaceful domestic scene in which Celie is piecing together a quilt she is making jointly with Sofia, symbol of co-operative effort among the women. Shug chooses to join Celie at her sewing, making Tobias the outsider in the group, and Celie for once has a sense of belonging: 'For the first time in my life, I feel just right.' This sense of security is one of Shug's most important gifts to Celie.

hair all cornrowed Done in a pattern of tight little plaits.

Letter 28 (p. 53)

The story line reverts to the troubles of Harpo and Sofia. Harpo has been furiously stuffing himself with food, six eggs for breakfast for instance. This letter reveals something of the married life of Harpo and Sofia, partly through Sofia's anxiety, partly through Celie's comments. A certain role reversal is natural to the two of them. Harpo really likes 'cooking and cleaning and doing little things round the house' while Sofia prefers heavy labour – field work, chopping wood or mending the roof. However, it is implied that Harpo is worried about his public image and the way his life is different from his father's, so, although he is only about half Sofia's size, he tries to put on weight. Ironically, since he seems to be worried about his feminine image, the fat he puts on attracts jokes about whether or not he is pregnant.

clabber Curds.
troth Trough (Celie's phonetic spelling again).

Letter 29 (p. 56)

Finally Harpo admits his problem over Sofia to Celie, who is a good listener and has most people's confidence, saying: 'I want her to do what I say, like you do for Pa.' However, as soon as he tries violence she blacks his eyes. Alice Walker wants to emphasize the difference between the marriages, and Celie spells out for Harpo the difference between his situation and hers: that Sofia actually loves him, and that she is simply not a woman who can be beaten into submission; similarly that the woman his father really loves is Shug, who would stand no bullying whatsoever. But Harpo cannot break out of the conventional thinking, 'The wife spose to mind,' and is merely sick. It is a situation which is both comic and tragic at the same time.

Letter 30 (p. 58)

To keep the balance, Sofia's point of view follows, when Celie visits her and explains what Harpo has said. She objects that she is getting tired of being treated in this way, and that Harpo wants not a wife but an obedient dog. She reveals another aspect of the problem: she no longer finds him sexually exciting, but what she really objects to is that he has not even noticed and 'heartfeeling don't even seem to enter into it.' It is probably this argument more than any other which attracts the reader's sympathy to Sofia, even though she is the one to break up the marriage. Celie, as conventionally minded as Harpo at this stage, assumes that a wife must stay with her husband however painful this may be; but Sofia has another answer, to leave. As before, her sister will support her, and she needs a holiday. This is what makes Celie deeply envious: 'Somebody to run to. It seem too sweet to bear.' Throughout the novel the mutual support of women is stressed, particularly the love of sisters, and this makes Celie's loss of Nettie the more poignant.

like running to the end of the road and it turn back on itself i.e. an emotional dead end because Shug is a woman.

Letter 31 (p. 60)

This letter shows Sofia's determination, as well as the support she derives from her sisters, who are all big strong girls who 'look like amazons'. Harpo's position is pathetic as he is deserted by his family, and we feel a certain sympathy for him as he changes the baby's nappy for the last time, wiping his eyes on it as he does so. Because it is a nappy, however, and because the baby gives a fart, the scene has a comic element as well.

seining fish Using a net which hangs vertically in the water and whose ends can be drawn together.
Dilsey, Coco and Boo Evidently the cows.

Letter 32 (p. 62)

In the six months which pass before the next letter, however, Harpo has ceased to be an object of pity. He has gained a new confidence; obviously he has a new friend whose identity is not yet revealed, and is full of plans for the future. This is the point where he constructs the jukejoint out of his old house. Faintly disreputable, this is in marked contrast to his previous rather weak conventionality. The fact that he manages so adequately means that we do not react to Sofia with dislike for deserting him.

Jukejoint Harpo's establishment appears to be merely a bar, or what we would call a jazz club, but some of these also functioned as brothels.

Letter 33 (p. 63)

It is Shug who breathes life into the jukejoint at last, demonstrating both her fame and her vitality in that she is able to do so. Celie is reluctantly allowed to go and watch her sing (the jukejoint is not respectable and Mr— tries to stop her, but Shug insists). This is an important stage in the developing relationship of Shug and Celie, because Celie is feeling rejected until Shug publicly names a song after her. The song itself seems of little relevance to Celie; there is irony in her lack of awareness of the possible significance of its title. But the feeling of being valued is a new experience for her and of immense importance.

chitlins Pigs' intestines, usually fried.
Bessie Smith (1898–1937) 'Empress of the Blues', a remarkable singer and woman of great presence. She was killed in a road accident and it is suggested that had she not been neglected because of her colour she might have survived. Edward Albee dramatized the incident in *The Death of Bessie Smith*.
sassy Cheeky.

Letter 34 (p. 66)

As Shug has now recovered from her illness, it is time for her to leave, but this letter shows that she now has a loyalty to Celie as well as Albert. Before she goes there is a tender scene between the two women, during which Celie reveals to Shug how Albert beats her 'for being me and not you'. Shug promises to stop him, and this is the second great service which she does for Celie in this part of the novel.

lightening bugs Fireflies.

Letter 35 (p. 68)

The next letter, however, shows that Celie also suffers because of Shug, who now regularly sleeps with Albert. (Celie does not care who Albert sleeps with, but she would like Shug for herself. Her jealousy is a measure of the intensity of her love.) The two women discuss their relations with Albert, and Shug is horrified to find that Celie has no pleasure at all in her relations with him, or with any man; 'you still a virgin', she says. She takes an important step in Celie's sexual education, by explaining to her how erotic response is caused and what it feels like.

not with my sponge and all This refers to an elementary method of contraception.

Letter 36 (p. 71)

When Sofia reappears, coming to the jukejoint, she is fuller than ever of vitality, with a prize fighter for a companion. It is part of her force of character that she is not the least bit disconcerted by what has happened to her home, and is perfectly prepared to have some fun. Mr— tries to force her into a conventional feminine role and shame her by asking where her children are, but Sofia has the perfect put-down: 'My children at home, where yours?' At this point the identity of Harpo's new woman, which had been hinted at before, is revealed. She is Mary Agnes, who is small and meek, but jealous of Sofia as she dances with Harpo. A fight develops between the women, which has its comic side, partly because it is so unequal. It also serves to remind us of Sofia's toughness and temper, which are to get her into trouble with the white people in the next episode.

white lightening Homemade, usually uncoloured, corn whisky.
teenouncy Impudent.

Letter 37 (p. 75)

The theme of race relations is further developed here, as the letter contains the story of Sofia's disastrous confrontation with the mayor's wife, Miss Millie. The problem arises, ironically, because Sofia and her children look attractive and self-sufficient. Miss Millie is taken with their appearance, and makes Sofia an entirely inappropriate offer to be her maid. Sofia does not take kindly to being patronized by anyone, and replies, 'Hell, no,' which leads to the mayor slapping her, and the scene develops into a fight. What is most clearly stressed here is the unfairness and severity of Sofia's treatment, and her helplessness against the ruling whites. Six policemen deal with the scene, which ends with Sofia being so badly beaten that Celie wonders why she is still alive.

sassing Cheeking.
eggplant Aubergine, a dark purple colour.

Letter 38 (p. 78)

The appalling severity of Sofia's punishment continues while she is in prison, condemned to work all day in the prison laundry. She has been sentenced to a horrifying twelve years. She has been reduced to the utmost subservience and her friends are deeply distressed by her physical and mental condition. It is the contrast with her previous strength and independence which is particularly painful.

roaches Cockroaches.

Letter 39 (p. 80)

Sofia's friends consider what can be done to help her, though the position at first seems impossible. They decide on an approach through the prison warden's black relatives; the stratagem shows how deep racial divisions are in Georgia. Mary Agnes here shows considerable generosity; in spite of her fight with Sofia she has been struggling to care for all the children.

She now admits that the warden is her uncle, which means that she will be the person to see him. Woman will help woman, even in spite of personal animosity, when there is real need.

God coming down by chariot A reference to the hope of salvation expressed in the Negro spirituals. Celie's tone is heavily ironic; God is white.

Letter 40 (p. 82)

The stratagem which is devised to help Sofia shows the relative positions of black and white people in this society very clearly, as well as the inherent meanness and corruption of the whites. Mary Agnes is dressed up as attractively as possible for the occasion, but her poverty is still apparent. The plan is not to ask for mercy for Sofia, but to pretend that being the mayor's maid would be a worse punishment for her than prison. The whites will then be bluffed into helping Sofia. It is significant that the success of the plot depends on whites behaving badly.

uncle Tomming Subservience to the whites. The expression originates from a character in the novel *Uncle Tom's Cabin: a Tale of Life among the Lowly* by Harriet Beecher Stowe (1852), which concerns slavery.

Letter 41 (p. 83)

In another episode of male corruption, cynicism and violence, the plan works, though at the cost of Mary Agnes being raped by her uncle (who is completely aware of what he is doing, but denies it). Coming home in a thoroughly dishevelled state, she gains, however, both in dignity and in Harpo's love by her sacrifice.

crackers The word originally meant outlaws or boasters, later white people of low status. Something of both senses may be intended here.
Shoot An exclamation common in southern dialect, meaning the same as 'Say,' in the previous sentence.
preshate i.e. appreciate.

Letter 42 (p. 85)

Mary Agnes now develops a talent for singing. The majority of the women in the novel have creative gifts of some kind. She is still angry with Sofia for the fight they had, but she understands Sofia's position in prison and cares for her children. (Sofia's sisters also help.) It is once again a case of mutual support among the women in the face of difficulties.

Letter 43 (p. 87)

Three years have passed before the next letter, during which time Sofia has recovered physically from her experiences in prison, but not mentally, because she 'just all time think bout killing somebody'. Life is very hard for her as the mayor's maid, a point which has the effect of stressing the low status of blacks in this society. Her job is to mind the children, and the six-year-old boy is allowed to order her about. His sister, Eleanor Jane, has an affection for Sofia, however, and is decent to her, so it shows that not all white people are totally obnoxious.

Letter 44 (p. 89)

Again there is a considerable time lapse before this letter, as Sofia has now served at least five years of her sentence, and again it concerns the attitude of whites to blacks. Sofia suggests that whites are actually inferior, or 'backward', in spite of their dominant position. As evidence she cites Miss Millie, the mayor's wife, and her incompetent efforts to learn to drive a car. As nobody else will teach her she is forced to ask Sofia; then, as a reward, promises her a single day at home to see her children. However, first she is not generous enough to let Sofia ride beside her in the car, forcing her to sit in the back; then she cannot actually manage to get home on her own. Sofia's time with her children lasts for fifteen minutes and she spends the rest of the day sorting out Millie's difficulties. Miss Millie fails on all counts here – she is as inept at handling the car as she is the social situation. Her attempted act of generosity to Sofia only shows how mean and limited she is.

clammed Climbed.

Revision questions

1 Comment on the relationship between Harpo and Sofia. How

far is this affected by the conventional ideas society has of how each sex should behave?

2 What comments has Alice Walker made about race relations in the story of the imprisonment of Sofia?

3 Many of the events described in *The Color Purple* are grim. How far do you think the novel also has its humorous side?

4 Why are relationships between sisters particularly important in *The Color Purple*?

Letter 45 (p. 93)

The story shifts into a new phase with the reappearance of Shug at Christmas. Both Albert and Celie are in a state of excitement, then Shug characteristically springs the totally unexpected on them – she is married to Grady. Celie's reaction to this new rival is succinctly expressed: 'Seem like to me he smell.' Grady is neither violent nor aggressive, but he is weak; this is another variant on male inadequacy.

Letter 46 (p. 95)

This letter is really a continuation of the last. There is a friendly intimacy between Celie and Shug, who now regards both Celie and Albert as 'like family'; but, although sympathetic to their difficulties with each other, she herself is oblivious of the pain she is causing them with Grady. Shug is becoming famous and doing well in every way, the model of the successful woman.

Sophie Tucker (1884–1966) Successful black singer and entertainer.
Duke Ellington (1899–1974) Famous American Negro jazz band leader and composer.

Letter 47 (p. 96)

It is only an illusion that Shug is out of reach to Celie, for after a short period of suspense the balance of the relationship shifts dramatically. While the two men are out, the women talk about love-making. Celie tells in pathetic and horrific detail the story of her rape by Alphonso. Although this was mentioned at the very beginning of the novel, Celie at that time was too young and too shocked to describe it as she does now to a sympathetic listener. She adds a little about her loveless marriage to Albert. Shug's instinctive reaction is to say 'I love you, Miss Celie' and to kiss her. This tenderness develops into the women making physical love to one another, and their relationship is to last the rest of their lives.

Letter 48 (p. 98)

Celie's delight at sleeping with Shug is broken into by the return of Grady; however, it now becomes apparent that the relationship of Shug and Grady is under a certain amount of strain already. For one thing he calls Shug 'Mama', which she strongly objects to; for another he clearly desires Mary Agnes. Shug shows considerable generosity here because, although she understands clearly that Mary Agnes is a sexual rival, she encourages her in her singing career. She appreciates the quality of Mary Agnes's voice, points out its potential, and offers to introduce her to the audience one night at Harpo's so that she has a chance to make an impression. It is another example of the generosity women show to one another in this novel, sinking personal rivalries when something important needs attention.

Swain come with his box i.e. an improvised jazz instrument.
preshation i.e. appreciation.

Letter 49 (p. 100)

The whole emphasis of the novel now shifts with the introduction of letters from Nettie. It is Shug, of course, who produces this transformation, the only character with the ability to do so; and she does it as a powerful gesture of her love for Celie. Having learned from Celie about the circumstances of Nettie's disappearance and her failure to send news, she connects this with Albert's mysterious behaviour at the mailbox, which Celie is never allowed to touch. The result is that Celie receives a short letter from Nettie containing some remarkable revelations. Nettie is not only alive, but so are Celie's children, Olivia and Adam, and they are thinking of returning to America soon. The very shortness of the letter increases its impact.

Letter 50 (p. 102)

This letter is more incoherent, dealing both with some of the
circumstances which led up to the previous one and with Celie's
subsequent reaction. The first part fills in how Shug managed the
affair from first learning about Celie's acute love for Nettie and
regret at not hearing from her. She apparently developed a great
friendliness with Albert, at the time causing Celie and Grady
painful jealousy. After a week, she was able to obtain from
Albert's pocket the letter which Celie has now read, so her real
loyalty was to Celie all the time.

Celie has always been represented as a character who is long-
suffering to a fault, but this is too much. The outrage is so great
that her meekness turns to violence. She quite seriously wants to
kill her husband for what he has done, and it is only Shug's
intervention which stops her cutting his throat with his own razor.
Shug nurses her through her shock, which is sufficient to make
her really ill, thereby returning one of Celie's earlier kindnesses
to herself.

As the women talk we learn more of Shug's early history, so
understanding the lack of affection from her mother, the way she
found consolation in the physical love she could have with Albert
(but no real support because he was too weak in character) and
the way church and society rejected her when she had illegitimate
children. Finally her parents turned her out and Albert married
someone else. It is a moving defence of the character's weak-
nesses. We see that Shug, too, has been a victim, deprived of the
love she needed. Particularly, she has been unfairly treated
because Albert's parents disapproved of her for having children
outside marriage, even though they were his children. However,
Shug is no saint. It is part of the attractiveness of the character
that she is spirited and a little wild. She did not let Albert go, and
carried on an affair with him even though his wife and children
suffered badly for it. She emphasizes how different her judgement of him is now from what it was in the early days. This is
important, because Albert has to appear credible both as Shug's
lover and as Celie's brutal husband, and there is a degree of
contradiction between the two. The problem is resolved by stressing first of all how much the relationship of Albert and Shug
depended on physical attraction, then how much he has changed
for the worse over the years. Later in the novel he is to change again.

buddy-buddy Extremely friendly.
reefer Smoking cannabis.
moochie A slow dance with the partners close together.

Letter 51 (p. 106)

This letter simply contains a little narrative, explaining how Shug and Celie secretly obtain Nettie's old letters from Mr—'s trunk.

Letter 52 (p. 107)

The next seven letters are all from Nettie, the oldest dating back nearly thirty years, and bringing us up to date with her story. First there is Mr—'s attempt to rape Nettie after he had ordered her out of his house, and Nettie's discovery of Celie's child.

Letter 53 (p. 108)

Next we have Nettie's involvement with Corinne, Samuel and the children. Her strong affection for Celie is very poignant, as is her urgent request for Celie to write to her.

Letter 54 (p. 109)

By this time Nettie has realized why there is no reply – Albert is concealing her letters. Again her loneliness is clearly expressed. This is the first mention of the missionary work in Africa which Corinne and Samuel are to undertake.

Letter 55 (p. 110)

This is the first of the series of detailed letters which Nettie writes; the previous ones have been short notes. Her style is clearly different from Celie's; more educated, with longer, more complex sentences and less use of black idiom. At this point the reader may well ask why Nettie is writing letters when she clearly realizes that they will not be answered, but the reason is a precise parallel with Celie's letters to God; they are an expression of almost unbearable loneliness.

The time scale is a little hard to follow here, as Nettie seems to have seen Sofia working as the mayor's maid. This would mean that at least six years elapsed between Nettie leaving Mr—'s house and going to Africa.

We learn the background of how she becomes a missionary, purely by chance. The dominant emotion conveyed in Nettie's first descriptions of her African experience is excitement. She is profoundly impressed by the scale and history of Africa, and of her own ignorance of it, while being most keen to learn. Intelligent, eager, and with few prejudices, she makes an excellent observer through whom fresh impressions of Africa can be conveyed. Nettie is also delighted by the opportunity she now has to watch over Celie's children.

Milledgeville, Atlanta Both cities in Georgia. Nettie's provincialism shows a little.

Letter 56 (p. 113)

Nettie's observations are wide ranging. This letter covers her thoughts and experiences in New York on her way to Africa. She considers the presentation of religion, and the way Jesus has been presented as white by white illustrators of the Bible, which is quite contrary to historical reality. Then this is placed next to mentions of the way white and black people are segregated: the way a white man makes an offensive remark about black missionaries going to Africa; the way the blacks in Harlem are extremely generous to the mission. It is all done without open comment, but the effect is to make the reader contrast the behaviour of blacks and whites to the disadvantage of the whites.

The Missionary Society itself is entirely white-dominated. Even the pictures on the walls are of white men. It seems ominous that it does not say anything of 'caring about Africa', but only about 'duty', and Nettie confesses to feeling depressed. This description is in fact the first preparation for the failure of the Mission later on. However, Samuel reminds the others that they and the Africans will be 'working for a common goal: the uplift of black people everywhere'. It is important that at this stage they feel a sense of kinship for the Africans.

Speke John Hanning Speke (1827–64), British explorer who discovered Victoria Nyanza and the headwaters of the Nile.
Livingstone David Livingstone (1813–73), Scottish missionary and

traveller. He explored widely in Africa and discovered, among other things, the Victoria Falls on the Zambezi.

Stanley Sir Henry Morton Stanley (1841–1904), explored Lake Tanganyika. He is famous for the incident where he 'found' Livingstone at Ujiji.

Letter 57 (p. 116)

Nettie's enthusiastic narrative continues with her experiences on board ship and in England. She praises what she can see in museums of the past culture of Africa, then briefly considers the part played by slavery in the history of that country and America. Nettie obviously considers slavery as one of the reasons for Africa's decline, because the people 'murdered or sold into slavery their strongest folks'.

J. A. Rogers This must refer to Rogers' *From Superman to Man* (Chicago, 1917) as his other major works were not published until the 1930s.

Letter 58 (p. 119)

The last letter of this series describes Nettie's actual arrival in Africa. It is full of descriptive detail of the physical appearance of the people, customs, scenery and economy, all carefully observed. Nettie's enthusiasm is summed up when she says that at the first sight of the African coast she 'just vibrated' like a large bell.

Revision questions

1 In what ways do Nettie's letters have an effect on Celie's life? Can you suggest reasons why Alice Walker introduces them at this precise point?

2 In what ways are the letter-writing styles of Celie and Nettie alike, and how are they different?

3 How favourable is the view of organized religion which is presented in the first half of the novel?

Letter 59 (p. 122)

Interest reverts to Celie and the main story line for the next two letters. Celie and Shug are brought closer together by the shock of Nettie's letters. Celie asks Shug to sleep with her for the rest of her visit. This in fact means that she is asserting a claim stronger than Albert's or Grady's.

Letter 60 (p. 124)

This letter is a continuation of the last. It is now that Shug has the important idea of getting Celie to make trousers, initially as therapy for the shock. It is also an important and symbolic gesture of independence.

Letter 61 (p. 126)

Celie's introductory paragraph reminds us of her anxiety over her children being conceived in incest (we are kept in suspense for several more letters before this matter is cleared up), then the rest of the letter concentrates on Nettie's arrival in Africa, which is described in detail.

It is plain from the beginning that the missionaries are complete outsiders to the Olinka, but at the same time Nettie is intensely sympathetic to their traditions. In particular, the discussion of the Olinka religion which occurs here is important, because the novel as a whole considers the different forms which religion can take and stresses the value of the spirit behind them rather than the observance of any particular set of traditional conventions.

Letter 62 (p. 132)

The feminist theme in the novel takes on a new development here, with a consideration of the position of the Olinka women, their relatively low status and their lack of education. An important parallel is also drawn between the attitude of Olinka men to women and that of whites to blacks in America. In spite of reservations on these matters, however, Nettie remains entranced with the Olinka culture in general. Her descriptions have the tone of an enthusiastic travel book. Alice Walker wants us to see and value the aspects of tribal Africa which are soon to be destroyed.

Tension between the characters is introduced with Corinne's growing suspicion and jealousy of Nettie, whom she tries to distance from Samuel and the children. Isolated as they are in Africa, this clearly has considerable potential for suspense and conflict in the story line.

Schweitzer Albert Schweitzer (1875–1965), theologian, musician and missionary. He gave up his career to found a leper colony at Lambarene in French Equatorial Africa.

Letter 63 (p. 136)

The specific disadvantages of the Olinka women are brought home to us through the experiences of one individual, Tashi, who is highly intelligent but undervalued by her people. She represents the struggles of the young in a changing world both here and later in the novel. The Olinka women are 'respected', as they see it, but there is a level of irony in this description because to an outsider this merely means that they are restricted. And Nettie's position as an outsider is heavily emphasized.

Letter 64 (p. 139)

There has been a time lapse of five years since Nettie first arrived in Africa. The extent to which this world really is changing now becomes apparent, with the incursion of a new road on the Olinka village. At first it seems harmless enough – merely progress and, ironically in the light of what happens later, the Olinka welcome it.

This letter also reinforces the themes of Corinne's jealousy of Nettie, and of the strength of friendships among women.

'Uncle Remus' Joel Chandler Harris collected the negro folk tales current among American slaves, making Uncle Remus the narrator and Brer Rabbit the most famous character. The first English edition was published under the title *Uncle Remus and his Tales of the Old Plantation* (London 1881). Tashi has heard an oral version of one of the stories which predates Harris's tales.

Letter 65 (p. 143)

In contrast to the earlier, cheerful description of the road, its real destructive power now becomes apparent. Its purpose is not progress for Africa but the exploitation of the land for the benefit of foreigners, and there is a strong sense of outrage at the violation of a whole way of life and disrespect for the rights of the Olinka tribesmen.

cut their eyes at i.e. looked suggestively. Compare Letter 12.

Letter 66 (p. 146)

Again the mood is sad. The whole of Nettie's world seems in decay, as Corinne's jealousy and conviction that the children must be Nettie's both grow, and the distress of the Olinka deepens.

Letter 67 (p. 148)

Unexpectedly, Corinne's obsession with Nettie's resemblance to the children produces a positive result. Samuel, too, has believed them to be Nettie's, and discussion of the subject brings out a revelation. Samuel used to be friendly with Alphonso: he knows the story of Nettie's parents. Most important of all is the fact that although Samuel had not realized that Alphonso was the father of Olivia and Adam, he knows for certain that he was not the father of either Nettie or Celie. They are the daughters of a man who was lynched by white people. Celie's anxieties about incest consequently prove to be groundless, although the story of her father's violent death is hardly less shocking and makes an important contribution to our understanding of the appalling state of race relations in the Deep South at that time.

Letter 68 (p. 151)

This letter is very brief indeed, to emphasize the extent of Celie's shock. It does, however, introduce Shug's decision to take her away to a new life, and so marks another turning point in the story.

Letter 69 (p. 152)

This is the first letter which is addressed to Nettie and not to God. It represents an important development, because now Celie has someone belonging to her, even though she still has many difficulties in her life. She now has the courage to return to her early home and face Alphonso, whose character is just as disreputable as ever. He is now on his third wife, a woman so young as to make Celie feel sick at the thought of it. He has also managed to continue Celie's father's business and make a success of it by corrupt methods, well-placed bribes and pay-offs. He is entirely unrepentant about his treatment of Celie, and so repulsive that, taking this portrait together with that of Albert, we find it very easy to understand her horror of men in general.

It is of course Shug, the loyal woman friend, who supports her through all this. In the scene which follows, where Celie tries and fails to find her parents' graves, Shug says significantly, 'Us each other's peoples now.'

cockleburrs Weeds with prickly seed pods.

Letter 70 (p. 157)

Nettie tells the truth about the children to Corinne, but she is unconvinced. Not all the women in the story are heroic, even though in general they behave better than the men.

Letter 71 (p. 159)

Through Nettie's recalling of details from the past, Corinne is finally convinced of the children's identity, and she admits her mistake on her death bed. So she does at least die with some dignity.

Letter 72 (p. 161)

Nettie is still very lonely here, but she finds consolation in the children and in her unswerving love for Celie. Her forgiveness of Corinne is also an attractive trait of character. Nettie's letters, with their high factual and descriptive content, often seem rather didactic. Alice Walker maintains our interest in her by stressing the love between the sisters. We also tend to identify with her compassion for the Olinka people, whose troubles are seen entirely through her eyes.

my friend comes A euphemism for a menstrual period.

Letter 73 (p. 164)

This is an extremely important letter, containing as it does the title phrase of the novel. Celie's disgust with men extends to God, because the image of Him which she has been brought up with is that of an old, white man, and both men and whites have been damaging to her. Shug shows her that this is a false image, and offers her an alternative. It is significant that this image is not external, but 'inside you'; that it is not based on gender, and that it is not condemnatory. Shug's religion is based on love and the enjoyment of beautiful things in creation, including 'the color purple'.

Although many of the other characters in the novel disapprove of Shug, they are all mean and narrow, whereas she herself has consistently been shown to be capable of deep love and warmth. It is her view, therefore, which carries conviction, because of her attractive personality. The terms in which she expresses the relations of God and humanity are deliberately vulgar, to stress that this God is not alien to ordinary people but part of everyday experience. This explanation is an important part of Celie's education, though initially she is too absorbed by her anger to take it in properly.

conked Hit over the head.

Letter 74 (p. 169)

Celie is now ready to assert her independence. The scene in which she does so is dramatic. Over dinner at Odessa's house she finds the courage to tell her husband, 'It's time to leave you and enter into the Creation.' For the first time in her life, she fights back. Possibly the location is significant. Odessa and Sofia, who is also present, have always been associated with women's rights.

Independence turns out to be catching. Mary Agnes declares her intention of leaving Harpo to become a professional singer. Sofia (out on parole from prison) tells Harpo both that her last child is not his, and that she is coming home for good. The effect is that of a mass uprising of the women against the men, who are left comically spluttering. It is not only Shug who supports Celie. Repaying earlier help, Sofia undertakes to look after Mary Agnes's child while she goes away.

bangs Fringe of hair.

Revision questions

1 What part does Mary Agnes play in the structure of the novel?

2 In what ways do we see Nettie's early enthusiasm for Africa modified over the years?

3 What do Nettie's African experiences contribute to the major themes of the novel?

Letter 75 (p. 175)

Another example of the unreliability of men is now given when Grady takes up with Mary Agnes. Albert's parting from Celie is as cruel as anything he has ever inflicted on her. He subjects her to a great deal of abuse, most of which is demonstrably not even plausible – rubbish such as 'this house ain't been clean good since my first wife died'. But the days when Celie would merely suffer are over for good; with the confidence that Shug has given her, she turns and curses him. Celie is beside herself, and we are given the impression that the curse will be effective. It is the turning point in her relations with Albert. In spite of all he could do to her, she has survived, to start a new life.

Letter 76 (p. 177)

Celie's existence in Memphis is a complete contrast. There is something childlike about the description of Shug's house, with its elephant and turtle motifs – a return to lost innocence. After a brief holiday from reality, however, both the women return to work. Shug goes back to her singing; Celie starts to make trousers. The atmosphere she now lives in, free from oppression and anxiety, brings out her creative talent. The trousers are original and desirable. They are also a symbol of her new equality with men. Most of the first pairs are given to women who have helped her, but Odessa's Jack, one of the few unobjectionable men in the novel, is not excluded.

souse Pigs' ears, trotters, etc., pickled for eating.

okra The pods of a plant used as a vegetable, sometimes known as ladies' fingers.

betsy bugs Strictly pinch bugs, but the term can be used of many small insects.

Letter 77 (p. 183)

The letter which follows is mainly an expression of Celie's confidence and happiness. She is now even able to take criticism (of the way she talks), evaluate and ignore it.

Letter 78 (p. 185)

The feminist theme comes to the fore again, in the issue of Sofia wanting to be a pall-bearer at her mother's funeral. She and her sisters are physically quite equal to this, but Harpo opposes it as unconventional. 'What it gon look like?' he asks. Celie reminds Harpo, humorously, of his past efforts to subdue Sofia, and the subject drops for the moment, only to be revived a little later. At the end of the letter Sofia has had her way and appears entirely justified.

This letter gives a measure of how far Celie has changed since the early days, when she was so inhibited. She introduces Sofia and Harpo to the smoking of cannabis, explaining that she uses it when she wants to make love or to talk to God, but that she has not needed it very much lately because 'me and God make love just fine anyhow'. Even the independent-minded Sofia is shocked by this statement, which sounds much more like something Shug might have said. It is a measure of the complete revolution in Celie's life, which Shug has brought about. The scene ends with all three characters smoking reefers, and listening to a humming noise they have become aware of, presumably the spirit of the universe which was there waiting to be discovered.

Letter 79 (p. 189)

Another startling effect of Celie's leaving home is described here in the transformation of Mr—, who has been changed into a

clean, industrious and even godly person – but not im
He went through a state of breakdown first, until H
and nursed him. This shows a man in a caring role; s
rare in this novel, but not neglected as a possibility. W
told that Mr— started to recover only after Harpo m̲a̲d̲e̲ h̲i̲m̲
return Celie's letters, which gives an almost supernatural force
to the curse she gave him when she left home.

Letter 80 (p. 192)

This is the longest letter in the series so far, mainly devoted to
Nettie's description of the troubles of the Olinka and her own
failure to find any practical solutions for them. Things have by
now reached crisis point for the Olinka, who are totally dispos-
sessed; they have moved to a barren stretch of land, and their
roofleaf has been desecrated. Nettie's sense of outrage is clear
through her description. When she goes to England for help,
however, she finds that the Missionary Society is more interested
in whether she and Samuel are married or not than in the fate of
the Africans, a piece of narrow-mindedness which totally defeats
Nettie. She does, however, marry partly as a result of it. But
Samuel says that the Africans 'hardly seem to care whether
missionaries exist' either. Christianity seems to have become
irrelevant to the matter of their tribal survival and identity.

The problems of the Olinka are most successfully brought
home in the dilemma of Tashi, whom Adam now loves. Tashi is
resigned to scarification of the face and to female circumcision
'to make her people feel better', even though she does not
believe in either custom because of her education. It is a
hopeless last gesture in the face of the annihilation of the tribe
by ruthless foreign interests.

This letter also contains a celebration of the adventurousness
of some of the women who went to Africa and elsewhere as
missionaries, though in the case of the most detailed story, that
of Doris Baines, the mission was merely an excuse for an unconventional adventure, an escape from a stultifying life at home.
Ultimately, however, their efforts are seen as futile and irrelevant, a matter of their own egotism more than anything else.

milked i.e. effeminate.
a bit of bloody cutting at puberty Female circumcision.
antimacassared Hung with protective and ornamental cloths.

The futility of Tashi's sacrifice is stressed here. After submitting to scarification she is infected and ashamed. Nettie and Samuel continue to do what they can in working for the tribe, but it is clear that there is no real way forward, that the past cannot be recovered or artificially preserved.

Letter 82 (p. 206)

Celie's fortunes take another turn for the good, as Alphonso dies and she discovers that his villainy in one way was worse than she imagined: the house he has been living in and the store which provided him with a good income should really have been hers all along. As a particular twist of irony his gravestone describes him as kind to the poor and helpless. It seems to her especially opportune that she now has her rights, because she has a home to offer Nettie if she returns to America. It seems as though Celie's step into independence is being rewarded in every possible way.

Letter 83 (p. 209)

But the happy ending does not come yet. Celie has more tribulations to go through before all her problems are resolved. The jubilation of the previous letter is only to provide a contrast with this, which shows how vulnerable Celie is even in her new life, because she is still dependent on Shug, and Shug now has a new lover. It is characteristic of Shug, that he is an unlikely man to choose, a boy of nineteen. (Shug seems to have a preference for men she can dominate.) The scene is set so as to bring out the full pathos of the situation. It takes place in a Chinese restaurant, which Celie loves, and is supposed to be a happy occasion. Shug makes the announcement over the fortune cookies and then asks for Celie's sympathy because she has 'just been dying to tell somebody', without reflecting on the tortures of jealousy she is inflicting on Celie. It is Celie's distress which is most emphasized. She is literally speechless, and writes notes to Shug to express her feelings. But the strength of her love is equally important; this will endure whatever Shug inflicts on her.

fortune cookies Sweets with a motto inside them.

flittish Effeminate.
buns Buttocks.
boocoos Lots of (from the French *beaucoup*).

Letter 84 (p. 213)

Another painful subject is now raised; Sofia's child, Henrietta, is fighting for her life, and in her concern over this Celie finds the strength to keep going. It is characteristic of her that it should be a generous concern for someone else which distracts her from her own misery. Albert is also concerned, and this makes the first link between him and Celie since their separation. The second is their mutual love for Shug, which begins to draw them together. Albert has been educated by his recent experiences. Now that Celie has stood up to him he makes a real effort to understand her. There is even the tentative offer of a second chance to make their marriage into a reality, but Celie explains her aversion to all men. 'Take off they pants,' she says, 'and men look like frogs to me.' His education has progressed so far that Albert actually seems to understand, because in a later letter it becomes apparent that he has humorously carved her a little statue of a frog.

Letter 85 (p. 216)

With the next letter it seems that the whole of Celie's brave new world has now collapsed around her, as she receives a telegram bringing the news of Nettie's presumed death at sea. Simultaneously her own letters to Nettie are returned unopened.

Letter 86 (p. 217)

In spite of the news of Nettie's death, the next letter is from her, leaving the question of what has really happened open for the moment, and creating suspense. Ironically, Nettie talks of coming home after nearly thirty years, and considers the problems of adjustment the children are likely to encounter. The letter itself is as gloomy as most others in this part of the novel, since at the end it suddenly relates how Adam is missing. He has run away to follow his friend Tashi into the forest, where she has presumably gone to join the rebels, Olinka society now being completely devastated.

Letter 87 (p. 220)

Celie's longest letter follows. It is written to Nettie, in spite of the telegram Celie received, and is a refusal to give up belief in her existence. A number of issues are raised.

Most of the space in this letter is devoted to Sofia and her relations with Eleanor Jane, the mayor's daughter. It is probably the most important examination of race relations in the novel, certainly the most detailed. There is some personal affection between Sofia and Eleanor Jane, as they have helped one another in the past, but the barriers of race still exist. Sofia refuses automatically to pretend to love Eleanor Jane's baby, Reynolds Stanley Earl, because she has her own troubles 'and when Reynolds Stanley grow up, he's gon be one of them.' Sofia's forthright honesty and her courage are stressed here, as well as the way it is Eleanor Jane, the white woman, who has the most to gain from the relationship. The scene ends with Eleanor Jane close to tears, but its total effect is not painful because of the descriptions of the baby, 'a little fat white something without much hair' and certainly without any dignity, who crawls on to Henrietta's bed looking as if he is 'trying to rape her foot'.

Contained within this letter is the substance of one from Shug, who is still living with Germaine and who has been to see her own children. The importance of this is that it leads to a further discussion between Celie and Albert about Shug and a remarkable depth of agreement between them about her qualities. 'It don't surprise me you love Shug Avery,' Albert says, 'I have love Shug Avery all my life.' He has recognized that forms of sexuality may vary from person to person, but that the love which finds expression in that way is essentially the same and cannot or should not be resisted just because society in general does not approve. It is one of the novel's most serious moral points.

As the scene develops, Celie and Albert embrace, 'two old fools left over from love, keeping each other company under the stars'. Albert actually helps Celie with her sewing, and listens to the stories of African mythology which she has learned from Nettie. The legends discuss the origin of men and of differences of colour and the bloodshed these have led to. Celie's telling of them reveals an anxiety that coloured people may fight among themselves as well as against the whites, unless one day everybody can accept everybody else as 'a child of God, or one mother's children, no matter what they look like or how they act'. This has an obvious bearing on her acceptance of Tashi and Adam at the end of the novel, ignoring the marks of tribalism scarred into their faces. Such a scene, with Albert peacefully accepting instruction and admitting that she is 'good company', is one of Celie's greatest triumphs.

snag that man i.e. catch, become engaged to.
cotton gin The machine which extracts the seeds from the cotton boll and separates them from the fibre.
cracker Biscuit.
messed over my first wife a scanless i.e. treated her shamefully.

Letter 88 (p. 234)

Adam and Tashi, their reappearance from the forest and Tashi's anxiety that she might be shunned in America, are the subject of the next letter. However, these difficulties are happily resolved, and Adam and Tashi are married. It is announced that Nettie and her family will soon be home, and although there is still a shade of ambiguity about whether they have survived or not, we are on the whole invited to be optimistic, given Celie's general mood at this point.

Adam Omatangu The end of the previous letter told the story of the first African, Omatangu, the equivalent of the Bible's Adam. Celie's Adam has now become an African, too.

Letter 89 (p. 237)

Another loose end is tied up; the conflict between Sofia and Eleanor Jane is resolved and ends in a real friendship. Eleanor Jane learns how Sofia came to work in her mother's house as a prisoner, and defies the prejudices of her family in order to offer real help to Sofia. In defiance of prejudice, it is shown that inter-racial friendship is possible.

Albert, as part of his new understanding with Celie, explains why he treated her so badly, out of disappointment that he could not have Shug. He has learned now to love, and is loved in return. Celie will not marry him again, but their differences are finally resolved in friendship.

Then Shug returns, the affair with Germaine being over at

last. Celie momentarily has the possibility of making Shug jealous of her new relations with Albert – yet another triumph – but generously rejects the temptation. All Celie's difficulties are now over except one.

It not my salvation she working for i.e. Eleanor Jane is doing good to herself, not Sofia, by her improved attitude to race.

Letter 90 (p. 242)

An ecstatic beginning marks the total reversal of Celie's fortunes. Once again this letter is written to God, but in celebration, not loneliness. The return of Nettie and the children completes Celie's happiness, and the novel ends with a family celebration, in total harmony.

make a lot of miration over i.e. greatly admires.

Revision questions

1 In how many different ways does the illness of Henrietta contribute to the structure of the novel?

2 What do we learn from the last part of *The Color Purple* about the relations of black Africans and black Americans?

3 Even after Celie is liberated by Shug, she still has some way to go to achieve complete independence. What do the last few letters in the series show about her continuing development?

Alice Walker's art in *The Color Purple*
The characters

Celie

You black, you pore, you ugly, you a woman. Goddam, he say, you nothing at all.

At the beginning of the novel Celie is a naïve and ignorant girl of fourteen and by the end she is well into middle age. It is the passing of her life which gives the book its structure, and naturally she develops and changes more than any other character. We watch her grow in knowledge of the world and in self-realization, and even her language changes and becomes more articulate as she develops confidence.

Her isolation in the beginning is appalling; her letters are addressed to God because she has literally no one else, and even her idea of God at this stage is of an old white man, very remote from her own experience. Those who ought to be her natural protectors have proved inadequate or abused their trust. Her mother, we learn later in the novel, became mentally unhinged by the violent murder and mutilation of her husband by white men who envied his success in running a dry goods store and in making a little money. She then married Alphonso and was further weakened by a pregnancy every year until she died shortly before Celie's own second child was born, not realizing that her husband raped and impregnated her daughter. Celie herself believes that Alphonso is her natural father and not her stepfather, having been only two years old when the murder happened, and is consumed with guilt at the thought that she has been forced to commit incest and must keep this a secret. Celie's children are taken from her in the most brutal way, without any indication of what has happened to them or even whether they are still alive. The only person in the world whom Celie has to love is her younger sister Nettie, and, far from offering support, Nettie in turn needs protection from Alphonso's lust. Then Nettie is forced to go away herself. The last person who might have been thought to have a duty towards Celie, her husband, is just as ruthless and exploitative as everyone else, and vindictively withholds Nettie's letters.

In the face of all this isolation and ill treatment Celie remains a 'good girl', kind, honest, dutiful and hard working. She is not particularly clever, having in any case been forced to leave school by her first pregnancy, but she has a strong desire to do right and possesses all the domestic virtues, being a 'good housekeeper, good with children, good cook'. Constantly stoical in the face of ill-treatment, and caring to the best of her ability for those weaker than herself, she protects Nettie from Alphonso's sexual advances by deliberately sacrificing herself. Then, when she is married to a man she does not even call by his first name (he is referred to as Mr— for most of the novel), she spends her wedding night trying to reduce his uncontrollable children to order and cleanliness. Her marriage is in fact virtual slavery, Mr— needing a housekeeper and being induced to take Celie, although he has a contempt for her, because a cow is thrown in as part of the bargain. Only once does Celie do something which is deliberately mean, and that is when she suggests to her stepson Harpo that he should beat his wife in order to make her do what he says. She does this out of jealousy because Harpo's wife, Sofia, is an entirely different character – big, strong and self-sufficient. However, Celie is so guilty about what she has done that she cannot sleep, and rapidly makes amends to Sofia. Eventually one of Celie's loving acts brings a reward, and that arises because she cares for Shug Avery when she is ill. Celie nurses Shug and skilfully tempts her to eat. As Shug recovers, this is the beginning of a relationship between the women which is to be the most significant of Celie's life.

Celie's relationships with men are disastrous. Possibly the least dreadful is that with Harpo, who is only a child in the beginning and not, in any case, a very virile character; but even he throws a rock at her the first time they meet and draws blood. After the early trauma of the rape she is understandably afraid of men and has no sexual desire for them at all. Her married relations with Mr— are simply something to be put up with. 'Take off they pants', she says, 'and men look like frogs to me.' But it is not either sexual brutality, or beating, or the constant demand for hard physical labour in cultivating the fields and looking after large numbers of her husband's children by other women that eventually drive her to fury. The time when she finally turns on Mr— is when she discovers how he has deliberately withheld Nettie's letters from her over the years. Then she definitely wants to kill him. When Celie finds the courage to stand up to

Mr— and to leave him, it is a sign that she has finally grown up. Eventually she reaches a sort of reconciliation with him, but only because she is now totally independent, earning her own living, and able to meet him on equal terms.

The only kindness Celie receives is from women and she repays this by deep love. She is still as loyal and as attached as ever to Nettie after thirty years of separation. Celie is not afraid of women; they do not brutalize or exploit her. She is immensely attracted by the idea of women as a refuge. For instance, when Sofia is tired of Harpo she goes to her sister, and Celie is intensely envious of such a relationship. 'Somebody to run to,' she says. 'It seem too sweet to bear.' When she eventually gets into bed with Shug it is the comfort she stresses: 'Little like sleeping with mama, only I can't hardly remember ever sleeping with her.' Celie's relationship with Shug is not, of course, totally comfortable. It makes her suffer acute pangs of pain or jealousy when Shug is capricious and particularly when Shug needs men. However, it is Shug who makes Mr— behave with a little more decency, and who enables Celie to achieve independence by encouraging her to sew trousers and providing the capital for her to go into business. It has been only a little support that Celie has needed all along, and when she gets it she is literally transformed so that her husband does not recognize her. The fact that her independence comes through the manufacture of trousers is of course symbolic. Celie is using a characteristically female skill in sewing, but she is now using it creatively, to make garments suggestive of male power and domination and which she wears herself as well as selling them. Her female role has never fitted her very well; dresses have never suited her, neither have they been suitable for the kind of life she has led. With what was once exclusively a masculine dress she has taken on a freedom of choice that was previously available only to men.

The realization of the nature of her own sexuality is something that comes to Celie very gradually. The reader picks up indicators that she is attracted to Shug long before she understands the nature of this attraction herself. She admires Shug physically, and it is the wish to look good before Shug which makes her conscious of her own appearance; but it is a long time before they actually make love. When they do Celie learns from Shug that sex is not something dirty and shameful but generous, an expression of delight and vitality. It is significant that the love

51

of God and the appreciation of what is valuable and beautiful in the world are seen in sexual terms. 'Lately I feel like me and God make love just fine,' Celie says at the point where she has resolved most of her problems.

Sexual liberation and economic liberation come together. 'I am so happy. I got love, I got work, I got money, friends and time,' she writes to Nettie late on in the novel. Money is something of which she has always understood the power. Early on she sends Nettie to Corinne for protection because Corinne is the only black woman she has ever seen with money. Economic independence gives her confidence such as she has never felt before in her life so that when one of her workers, Darlene, criticizes her uneducated speech she is able to evaluate the criticism and ignore it. (It is also, of course, that she now feels confidence in Shug's love.) It seems as though by taking charge of her own life she has also changed her luck, because Alphonso now dies and Celie inherits from her real parents substantial property, which should have come to her before, but which Alphonso had withheld. From being totally subservient she now becomes dominant. She will have a suitable home to offer Nettie and the children on their return from Africa, and when Nettie and the children finally do return her happiness is complete. Even Mr— is included in the general happiness, being admitted as family in general – though not as a husband – and referred to as Albert to indicate that he is mostly forgiven.

Shug Avery

The Queen Honeybee.

Shug is short for 'Sugar'; her real name is Lillie but 'she just so sweet they call her Shug' or sometimes the 'Queen Honeybee', not as an alternative nickname but more as a tribute to her artistry and her hold over the personalities with whom she comes into contact. Shug is a Blues singer, and appears to be partly based on the great Bessie Smith, who is mentioned in the novel and whom Shug is supposed to have known.

The dominant impression of Shug Avery is of an immense vitality. If she is sweet, she is certainly not saccharine, for she can be difficult or capricious at times. This is Celie's first impression of her: 'She sicker than my mama was when she die. But she more evil than my mama and that keep her alive' – with a little help from Celie's nursing, that is. Her first defiance in adult life was against her parents, who finally threw her out after her third illegitimate child (all by Albert, later Celie's husband). When she heard that Albert was married to his first wife, Annie Julia, it did not make a scrap of difference; she describes herself as being so 'mean' and 'wild' that she made love to him just the same, totally careless of anyone else's opinion or of Albert's neglect of his children, and she came back to him at intervals throughout her life. It is not just that she disregards convention, however. She causes real pain to others' feelings by the pursuit of her own desires. For example, she insists on telling Celie all about her passion for Germaine, towards the end of the novel, oblivious at first that Celie is suffering extreme jealousy, because 'I just been dying to tell somebody, and you the somebody I usually tell.' She does, however, respond to Celie's distress afterwards.

Germaine, who is a boy of nineteen – Shug is three times his age – is only the last of a long series of love affairs. In early life Shug's problems with her mother stemmed from the fact that her mother was a woman who disliked physical contact of any kind: 'One thing my mama hated me for was how much I love to fuck,' she tells Celie. She has a very powerful sensuality. Shug's affair with Albert lasted for a long time because it was so physically successful that she felt it was a good example of the way nature intended sex to be, even though she knew very well that he was a weak man all the time and later came to disapprove of his moral character. Grady, her husband, is also a weak character in a different way. In all her love affairs Shug is, for one reason or another, the dominant partner.

In fact, although she is described as a physically attractive woman with a strong sexuality and a taste for alluring clothes, there is always a certain air of masculinity about her. She wears furs and rouge, tight dresses 'all up her leg' and low necklines. She positively adores heterosexual love-making. But there is something about the way she is in charge, something in her freedom and her manner of speech, that makes Celie notice 'how Shug talk and act sometimes like a man'. It is not only Celie who has this impression; Albert, too, says that 'Shug act more manly than most men.' By this he means that she is honest, open and direct. So it comes as no surprise when her affection for Celie finds a physical expression; the lesbian tendencies are not in Celie alone, and the two complement each other emotionally.

To Celie, Shug is a great source of strength. Shug's morality may not be conventional but she does not approve of brutality. She makes Albert stop beating Celie, and even attempts to make him behave a little better to her in bed. When Celie's resentment of Albert comes to a head over the discovery that he has hidden Nettie's letters, it is Shug who gives Celie what she has always wanted – an escape route, taking her away to Memphis and supporting her financially as well as emotionally until Celie is able to support herself. Shug stands for freedom and fulfilment, having a generosity of spirit that the men in this novel noticeably lack. This is not only shown in relation to Celie: Shug encourages and advises Mary Agnes to take up a professional singing career even though this also means that Mary Agnes eventually elopes with Shug's husband, Grady. Shug is perfectly well aware of Grady's desire for Mary Agnes, but does no more than tell him so.

It is Shug who is given the most important of the thematic concerns in the novel which relate to sex and to religion. She has important things to say about both. Shug teaches Celie the distinction between sexual experience in the mechanical sense and the full enjoyment of sexuality as an expression of delight in life. She tells Celie, who has never experienced sexual pleasure, that she is 'still a virgin' in spite of her two children, and gives her a frank and delighted account of what she is missing. Sex, for Shug, has a kind of holiness. 'God love all them feelings,' she says, 'That's some of the best stuff God did.'

What she most firmly rejects is a God who is white, male, and puritanical. She rejects the conventional Church because it is precisely this distorted image which is found there. Shug's religion is a kind of sympathy with nature and with humanity: 'God is everything' in her view and to be found both within ourselves and in the natural world. The 'color purple' of the title is her example of the richness of creation, and the proper reaction to it is one of admiration and joy. She refers to God in terms that some would find irreverent and even shocking, saying that 'it pisses God off' when its (not His) surprises and delights are ignored. There is something very childlike about this religion, simplistic but sincere.

There is something childlike about Shug in other ways, too, in spite of her superficial sophistication of money, power and tight dresses. She carries Celie off in the end to an enormous house decorated with elephant and turtle motifs. She has visions of another house, entirely round and pink, 'like some kind of fruit'. It is perhaps this and her occasional sense of humour that make Shug such an engaging character. Restraining Celie from killing Albert, she says, 'Miss Celie, if you kill Albert, Grady be all I got left. I can't even stand the thought of that.' She appears, for most of the novel, to give little thought to her three children; she takes up with Albert at intervals and then disappears again; she leads an irresponsible, nomadic existence in many ways. But through it all there is a simple human warmth and a love, which is what attracts others. For Celie she ends up as the ultimate expression of family closeness, mother, sister and lover all rolled into one, and she herself expresses this at the point where Celie has finally learned her own early history but failed to find her parents' unmarked grave: 'Us each other's peoples now.'

Alphonso, Albert and Grady, and other male characters

Wherever there's a man there's trouble!

The men are all differentiated to some extent, but they have one thing in common – their inferiority to the women. Almost all of them behave deplorably because of their essential weakness. There are male characters in the novel who are brutal, but with one exception they are not actually strong: that is the women's role.

Alphonso, whom Celie and Nettie call 'Pa' in the beginning, is the least attractive, violating his fourteen-year-old stepdaughter on the first page of the novel then for some strange reason making her cut his hair at the same time. What he stands for is men's crude sexual voraciousness. He takes Celie because his mentally fragile wife at least has the strength to refuse his advances immediately after she has had yet another child. His taste for very young women seems to verge on the sexual perversion of paedophilia, because not only does he rape Celie but also has clear designs on the even younger Nettie; his second wife, May Ellen, went back to her people because she 'got too old for me, I reckon'; and his last wife, Daisy, is aged fifteen. He dies in Daisy's arms and is buried under a magnificent tombstone that ironically describes him as 'an upright husband and father'.

Alphonso's lust is matched only by his hypocrisy. He retains the inheritance which should have belonged to Celie and Nettie and uses it to build up a successful business, while handing over Celie as a virtual slave to his friends. He admits that 'she ain't fresh', but totally conceals that he himself is the father of her children. Later he implies that he kept the truth about their father's murder from Celie and Nettie in order to protect them from shock, claiming, 'Any man would have done what I done.'

Albert, known through much of the novel as Mr— because Celie is not even on friendly enough terms with him to use his first name, is a slightly more complex portrait, but sufficiently similar to Alphonso for them to understand one another very well. His marriage to Celie is more or less a commercial transaction. He actually preferred Nettie, but is persuaded to take Celie because he needs a mother for his children and a hard worker for his fields. He then systematically beats her 'Cause she my wife.' It is a portrait of total callousness and exploitation.

His slightly more attractive side emerges in relation to Shug. Albert, though rather a small man, is supposed to be physically good looking; though constantly described as a weak man, he has a profound passion for Shug which lasts a lifetime. When Shug is ill he genuinely suffers extreme pangs of anxiety, and this makes him seem a little more human, together with the fact that, according to Shug, when he was young he would laugh and dance and make love with enthusiasm. In middle age he has become mean and vindictive. What Celie considers his most cruel act is to keep Nettie's letters from her. This he does as an act of revenge because Nettie rejected his sexual advances.

Albert's attitudes towards women are authoritarian. He tries to stop Celie going to the jukejoint to hear Shug sing, on the grounds that, 'My wife can't do that.' He is not beyond redemption, however, when women stand up to him, and begins to behave a little better to Celie when Shug tells him to. Eventually, when Celie curses and leaves him, he suffers a breakdown through guilt, but Harpo helps him, and he recovers after making what amends he can to Celie by sending her Nettie's letters. After he has become properly submissive he and Celie get on better than might have been expected; not sleeping together, but united in their love for Shug.

Grady shows a different kind of weakness. He is really just a temporary appendage to Shug and is subtly repellent, with his large teeth, red suspenders and bow ties. Shug comments unfavourably on his sexual prowess: 'I don't know who tried to teach him what to do in the bedroom, but it must have been a furniture salesman.' Less violent than the others, he is just as partronizing to women. When Celie is leaving Albert, Grady remarks that it will damage her reputation: 'A woman can't git a man if peoples talk.' This rightly attracts laughter, especially as, ironically, he elopes with Mary Agnes soon after. Grady is just as unscrupulous over the seduction of women as all the other men, only gentler by nature. He ends up growing cannabis on a considerable scale, making plenty of money, but mostly stoned out of his mind.

Among the subsidiary characters, there is a tendency for the men to be either violent, like Sofia's prize fighter, or ineffectual, like Shug's flute player, Germaine, who is talented but slightly effeminate and only nineteen years old. The only male character of any moral standing is Samuel, the missionary, whom Nettie eventually marries. The presentation of the men has a cumulative effect throughout the novel. Even God, while thought of as male, shares in the general opprobrium and is at one stage described by Celie as 'just like all the other mens I know. Trifling, forgitful and lowdown.'

Sofia and Harpo

The woman that brought Sofia in the world brought something. Strong in body but weak in will.

Only one of Mr—'s children, Harpo, plays any significant part in the novel, although Celie spends some years looking after them. Harpo's character is more developed because of the nature of his relationship to Sofia, which Alice Walker uses to introduce the idea of a degree of role reversal, though probably the focus is more on Sofia's masculine tendencies than on Harpo's feminine ones.

Even at the age of fifteen, when she marries, Sofia is a formidable character. Her first appearance is symbolic of the nature of their relationship: she comes up to the house with Harpo 'marching hand in hand, like going to war. She in front a little.' She remains in front a little throughout their marriage. As with so many of the women in this novel, Sofia is heavily pregnant when she marries, but she is no victim. She has made a choice and is well able to cope with the consequences; partly because she has the support of sisters; partly because she is a big, strong woman, full of robust health and well able to stand up for herself in a physical fight.

Sofia likes heavy, outdoor work, like chopping wood to make shingles for the roof. Harpo turns out to be a good cook, and does domestic things well. When his father is ill towards the end of the novel, Harpo cares for him tenderly. The trouble arises because Harpo is too conventionally-minded just to accept this division of labour and enjoy having a wife who loves him and his children. 'The wife spose to mind,' he says, comically bursting into tears because he cannot beat his dutiful wife who blacks his eyes if he tries to do so. Even more comically, he stuffs himself with food in an attempt to put on enough weight to take her on in a physical fight. A similar issue arises when Sofia and her sisters claim the right to be pall-bearers at their mother's funeral. Women are supposed to be weaker, he argues, 'Cry if you want to. Not try to take over.' Naturally, he loses again, and when Sofia gets her own way, this is totally accepted by the congregation at the funeral.

Part of the plot of the novel is provided by Sofia's misfortunes when she goes to gaol for a conflict with the mayor's wife. It begins with a simple refusal to be patronized and to work as the mayor's wife's maid. The refusal turns into a violent battle during which Sofia is severely beaten up and eventually forced to be grateful for the job during her twelve-year prison sentence, because the alternative is unendurable living conditions in gaol. The main point of all this is to show the vicious attitude of the ruling whites to the blacks. All Sofia has done is to behave impulsively, to show proper pride and natural indignation, yet even her strength is humbled. She is expected to love those who have humiliated her, but retains enough dignity not to do so. All through her imprisonment and even afterwards she cares conscientiously and politely for Eleanor Jane, the mayor's daughter, but adamantly refuses to love Eleanor Jane's baby, or to even pretend to do so. 'Some colored people so scared of whitefolks they claim to love the cotton gin,' she says, but will not pretend to what seems to her a dishonest reaction. Eleanor Jane finally takes the point, and is then rewarded with friendship instead of the ability to patronize.

Much of the plot depends on the marital difficulties of Sofia and Harpo. In the beginning they love one another but then Sofia tires of Harpo; what she really resents is that Harpo does not even notice that she no longer desires him. Their lives follow separate courses. Sofia's independence is somewhat humbled by her long spell in prison. Harpo is distressed when his wife leaves him, but shows a turn for originality and enterprise by turning his house into a jukejoint when his domestic life temporarily ceases. (This, of course, provides a link with the Shug Avery strand of the novel.) Each of them has other affairs and children by other people, but they finally accept one another's needs and peculiarities, reaching a satisfactory balance in caring for their assorted children.

Mary Agnes (Squeak)

Squeak, Mary Agnes, what difference do it make?
It make a lot, say Squeak. When I was Mary Agnes I could sing in public.

Mary Agnes is a minor character, but she does again show the potential and the individuality of women. Harpo takes up with her when his wife leaves him, and it looks for a moment as though she is going to be another classic victim. She is small, does anything Harpo says, and finds looking after Sofia's children while she is in prison something of a strain. What she shows, though, is the generosity of women towards one another. Her uncle (white) turns out to have enough influence to get Sofia out of prison, and Squeak joins in a scheme to get him to use that influence, although the uncle rapes her in the process. She turns out to be another woman with a creative talent – for singing this time – having a voice 'sort of like panthers would sound if they could sing'. In defiance of Harpo, who burbles, 'Everything you need I done provided for,' she joins in the general female assertion of independence, opting to go north to be Mary Agnes the singer instead of staying at home in her less dignified domestic role of Squeak. She is given crucial support by the other women, by Shug for assistance in her musical career, and by Sofia in looking after the child she has by Harpo. Not all her actions are heroic, as she elopes and takes to cannabis farming with Grady, but she eventually both achieves success and returns to care for her daughter.

Nettie and the family in Africa

Nettie's history plays a most important part in the novel, and she embodies one of the major themes: the relationship of black African to black American experience. She also has some things to say about religion, and she is, of course, the person who ultimately brings up Celie's children. In spite of all this, however, she never seems so fully developed a character as the other women, possibly because many of her letters are descriptive or discursive as well as personal. Nettie is the clever one of the family, a great reader with a thirst for education; she therefore writes a different kind of prose from Celie, with longer, more complex sentences (but not so lively).

Physically, Nettie is supposed to resemble Celie, but she is considered to be more attractive. The attractiveness, of course, exposes her to unwanted sexual advances from both Alphonso and Albert, and forces her to leave home in order to escape degradation. The character traits which she has in common with Celie are perhaps her strong sense of duty and family loyalty. She never stops writing to Celie at Christmas and Easter, even though she knows that the letters have little chance of being delivered, and she regards it as a 'miracle' that she is able to watch over Celie's children: 'To lavish all the love I feel for you on them.' Another thing which the sisters have in common is their isolation and loneliness, for Africa, where she is a permanent outsider, always remains an alien society to Nettie, and Corinne, the woman who has adopted Celie's children, is suspicious of her. Nettie remains remarkably understanding and forgiving in spite of Corinne's sexual suspicion and jealousy of Nettie's entirely blameless relations with her husband, Samuel. Eventually, Nettie's patience and tolerance are rewarded, after Corinne's death, by her own marriage to Samuel, but there is not the least hint of sexual attraction between the two while Corinne is still living.

Samuel is the only man in the novel who could possibly be regarded as a desirable husband. He is a big man, of sombre appearance except for 'the most thoughtful and gentle brown eyes', and is invariably considerate and charitable. His failure as a missionary is bitter to him and it is in comforting him that Nettie declares her love. So even here it is the woman who displays most of the initiative. Samuel and Corinne, who are both educated, are the means of enlarging Nettie's horizons, through their information and in the most literal sense by travel, and so widen the scope of the novel. As they are both missionaries, and introduce Nettie to the missionary way of life and thought, their attitude to religion makes a telling counterbalance to Shug's as well as to the religion of the Olinka among whom they work.

Nettie also acts as a substitute mother to Celie's children, Adam and Olivia, and in fact it is the physical resemblance between the children and her which is the original ground of Corinne's suspicious behaviour. They remain 'children' and Nettie's attitude remains that of watchful responsibility throughout the novel, even though by the end of it Adam and Olivia are in their thirties. (They marry a little later than most of the other characters.) Nettie's careful, anxious account of the children's problems colours the whole way African society is presented in the novel. She is particularly sympathetic to the problems of women in Africa, identifying the anti-feminist attitudes of the Olinka men with those of the white people towards the coloured back home, so she has a particular care also for Tashi, the African girl who becomes Adam's wife. Nettie's role is that of the attentive, understanding observer, making little of her own difficulties, but deeply sympathetic towards those she loves. We feel that she deserves the happy ending when she is allowed the comfort of a suitable marriage and a return home.

Themes

Feminism

'Men spose to wear the pants,' says Albert when he finds out how Celie has been spending her time since leaving him, and it is meant, of course, both literally and symbolically. Both in Georgia and in West Africa, Alice Walker describes intensely male-dominated societies and the struggle women inevitably have to gain decent treatment.

We become aware of male dominance very early in the novel, in the form of sexual aggression. The first letter contains an account of Alphonso's rape of Celie. When Mary Agnes helps Sofia get out of prison she is raped by her own uncle. Mr— makes an attempt on Nettie, and only lets her go because she fights and manages to hurt him. With such a background, it is hardly surprising that Celie sees men as frightening. She lives in a society which tolerates and expects male violence. Even Harpo, who really loves his wife, decides to hit her because 'the woman spose to mind'. In his view, it is positively respectable to beat your wife.

Women are also seriously exploited. Mr— marries Celie because he cannot manage his children himself and needs domestic help. In bed, he treats her no better than a prostitute: 'Never ask me how I feel, nothing. Just do his business, get off, go to sleep,' she says, pathetically. It is she who ploughs and does heavy farm work. Celie's treatment is all too typical. Alphonso's second wife may have a little more pleasure sexually, but she is just as defeated by the demands of his children as Celie is by her own husband's: 'he got so many of us. All needing somethin,' Celie writes.

An attitude of superiority is so ingrained in the men that they are not even aware that they are being objectionable. This may be seen clearly in the milder-mannered of them. Harpo eventually has to accept that he cannot beat Sofia in a fight, but he still mistakenly tries to stop her being a pall-bearer at her mother's funeral. When Mary Agnes tells him that she wants to pursue her career as a singer, his reaction is, 'Everything you need I done provided for,' just like the Olinka men with their 'respect' for women. Told that Sofia's youngest child is not his, he understandably orders, 'Go git me a cool glass of water,' and then, remembering his real position of weakness, is forced to add 'Please'. Grady, on being told that Celie and Mary Agnes are going away because they want independence, totally fails to take in the implications and burbles, 'A woman can't get a man if peoples talk,' and is rightly greeted with gales of laughter. That women should actually want to manage by themselves is beyond his limited comprehension. Being patronized by men is not as damaging as suffering physical violence, but it is all part of the same set of attitudes of dominance, even though the degree of callousness is less.

The novel's message is that women must stand up against this, and that they must help one another. It is impossible to dominate Sofia because from an early age she has learned to fight. She has to: 'A girl child ain't safe in a family of men,' she says. But Sofia is unusual in that she has not only great force of character but physical strength. The other women co-operate with one another, as does Sofia herself. There is a great stress laid on the bond between sisters, between Celie and Nettie, Sofia and Odessa. Others help out of friendship, or loyalty. Mary Agnes does her best to help Sofia when she is in prison, and in return Sofia looks after Mary Agnes's child when she goes away to be a singer. It is Mr—'s sister who puts in a good word for Celie. Olivia supports Tashi. In Africa the women have strong friendship groups among themselves, although they are undervalued by the men. The liberation of Celie by Shug is the emotional core of the novel. Alone, many of the women are weak; united, their force is more than equal to that of the dominating men.

Besides supporting one another, the women also try to break out of their subservient position by questioning traditional roles. The Sofia–Harpo relationship is the most obvious. It is Sofia who does the heavy outdoor work, like putting shingles on the roof, whilst Harpo enjoys domestic tasks. But while Sofia is well adjusted to this defiance of convention from the beginning, Harpo has a hard job to learn to accept it. That Celie's business enterprise turns out to be making trousers for women is, of course, no accident. It is a declaration of equality. Sewing, however, is still conventionally a feminine business, and men must be taught to appreciate its value. The moment when Mr— is finally reconciled with her and becomes a companion – 'someone I can talk to' – is the moment when he helps her stitch some pockets into the pants she is making and admits that he likes doing so. The first step towards equality is the freedom to leave, and that means that the women must be able to support themselves. 'Git a job,' Sofia suggests to Eleanor Jane when she begins to talk about the difficulties of her marriage. Beyond that again, however, lies the struggle for respect, and the men have to be made to adjust their attitudes to admit that the women are capable and that their work is of value.

There is also some discussion of masculine and feminine qualities of temperament, mainly associated with Shug. Mr— describes Shug as 'more manly than most men. I mean she upright, honest.' She is independent and confident of her own integrity. Celie agrees about Shug possessing these qualities, but denies that they are masculine ones. 'What Shug got is womanly it seem like to me,' she says. Her point is that these qualities are not actually linked to one sex, but belong as personality traits to individuals. Some men are weak and some women are strong. Relationships in the novel are happy only when they recognize this and allow individuality to develop, but restriction is liable to bring disaster. 'If you hadn't tried to rule over Sofia the white folks never would have caught her,' Celie tells Harpo.

In this novel it is mostly the women who are strong. Alice Walker's sympathetic womanism makes her select and emphasize female characters who are more admirable than the male (these being decidedly inferior, taken as a group). Odessa's Jack, a very minor character, is agreeable enough; Samuel is gentle and good: and Mr— is in part forgiven and rehabilitated towards the end; but it is the women in the novel who have both creative talent and insight. Celie, Shug, Sofia and Mary Agnes all end fulfilled and triumphant through their own efforts. Only Nettie ends as a conventional wife. Even the romantic interest is unfavourable to men. The greatest love, the most powerful emotional force in the novel, comes from the love between two women, between Celie and Shug. This love is not only the deepest; it is also the most complex and the longest lasting. It includes both sexuality and support.

Racial tensions

Celie's defenceless position in the world can ultimately be traced back to a racial incident. It was because her father was prosperous as a farmer and store-keeper that he excited the envy of white merchants near by, and so he was lynched by white men and his store burned down. He had committed no other offence than that of being successful, but that was enough to destroy him and his family.

A sense of racial tension runs through the whole of this book, as it does through all Alice Walker's work. Sometimes it comes out in quite small indications, casual remarks, as when Shug learns of Celie's dreadful early life and rape by her stepfather, and says, 'Wellsah, and I thought it was only whitefolks do freakish things like that.' There is an automatic assumption that the blacks will be poor, so that Mary Agnes is dressed up at her most attractive 'like she a white woman, only her clothes patch'; or Celie, seeing the magnificence of her inherited property, says, 'Us must have took a wrong turn ... This some white person's house.' There are small details such as that of the coloured people having a separate cemetery, details which are not at all stressed, but which are reminders that this is a segregated society. And there is the occasional deeply offensive remark, such as that of a bystander during Nettie's early days as a missionary: 'Niggers going to Africa ... Now I *have* seen everything.'

It is, however, the story of Sofia which is specifically shaped to show the hazards of being a black person living in Georgia. Sofia is spirited and strong, yet she is reduced to total helplessness when she comes into conflict with the mayor's otherwise ineffectual wife, who just happens to have the power of the white ruling class behind her. The whole point is that Sofia is in a car (a rare status symbol in those days) and 'looking like somebody'. In refusing an entirely inappropriate offer to go and do menial domestic work for the mayor's wife all she is doing is refusing to be patronized. For this she is first slapped, then, when she loses her temper and retaliates, severely punished, although it was not she who struck the first blow. After a bad enough beating she is glad when her friends manage, by a trick which depends on exploiting the ill nature of those in power, to get her the position of maid which she so despised before. And her standing then in the household is so low that she can be ordered about by a six-year-old child.

The severity of the beating Sofia gets, the length of her sentence, the way Miss Millie and even Eleanor Jane are free to patronize and make unreasonable demands on her, all these are represented as being entirely owing to her colour – natural results of the normal attitude of whites towards blacks in this society. Sofia's Christmas visit to her children shows clearly the ingrained selfishness of the white attitude. Miss Millie thinks she is being genuinely kind to Sofia in taking her to visit her family, but when she cannot manage her car by herself her own convenience is much more important than Sofia's visit. It is the details which are so telling: Sofia cannot sit beside her in the car, but must get in the back as an inferior. Offered a perfectly good lift home from Sofia's sister and brother-in-law, Millie says she cannot possibly ride with 'a strange colored man', and insists on Sofia's abandoning the visit. And then at the end she expects Sofia to be grateful.

It is perhaps the attitude of the whites which rankles most, even more than the blacks' economic disadvantages. The blacks are often trapped by poverty and poor education, but for the energetic and independent there are at least partial success stories. Celie's father did have a thriving business, so did Alphonso after him. Shug makes money as well as being a success in artistic and creative terms. Celie herself eventually becomes prosperous through work and talent. But even the incompetent whites consider themselves superior to talented blacks. 'They have the nerve to try to make us think slavery fell through because of us,' says Sofia. 'Like us didn't have the sense enough to handle it.' They think they can address someone as strong and resolute as Sofia as 'auntie' – although it has to be said that in her case they only try it once.

It is a background of deeply ingrained prejudice, and, like most prejudices, the harder to fight because it is unconscious. In the end this is not a pessimistic novel, however, and there is one clear case where the racial tension is resolved. Again, Sofia is concerned, here in her relationship with Eleanor Jane. From childhood, Eleanor Jane had an affection for Sofia, who brings her up and continually takes the trouble to help her with her problems. Yet eventually there is a confrontation between the two of them: Eleanor Jane makes constant demands on Sofia, but does not actually treat her as an equal. When she also demands Sofia's love for her child, there is a rebellion.

Sofia admits that Eleanor Jane has some claim on her for past kindnesses, but absolutely denies that this extends to loving the baby (who is vigorously messing up her house at the time). First Sofia seems to object to being seen as one of a class, not an individual. 'All the other colored women I know love children,' says Eleanor Jane, but Sofia points out that this is simply because as a race they are used to being intimidated, and that 'Some colored people so scared of whitefolks they claim to love the cotton gin.' The second issue which Sofia raises is that the baby is going to grow up with the prejudices of his race and class. His mother will not be able to stop him being 'mean to colored' because she will not be strong enough to counterbalance the prejudices of society. Alice Walker ends this little scene with Eleanor Jane rejected and close to tears.

That is not the end of the relationship, however. Eleanor Jane makes an effort. She finds out Sofia's past history and, having understood that, creates a real friendship on equal terms. Instead of just demanding attention for her own child, she offers positive help in looking after Sofia's daughter Henrietta. She does actual work in preparing food that Henrietta will accept – a bizarre concoction of yam ice cream. The significance of this is that it creates a sensation among her family, who begin 'carrying on just like you know they would. Whoever heard of a white woman working for niggers, they rave.' But Eleanor Jane has an appropriate answer: 'Whoever heard of somebody like Sofia working for trash?'

This resolution of the conflict is not, of course, typical. It is extraordinary. What is typical is the attitude which sees the blacks as inferior in every way. But the incident is given a good deal of space, and is placed in a significant position at the climax of the novel as part of the general happy ending. It is worth discussing in detail because it has a moral force, and shows that understanding is possible with goodwill on both sides, even though the State of Georgia still has a long way to go before that understanding becomes at all common.

Religion

It is a passage dealing with religion which gives the novel its title, and this subject receives a good deal of consideration in the course of the various letters. Celie's changing attitudes to religion are an important part of her emancipation, as she rejects the conventional institutions of the Church for something much freer. Nettie's view, too, broadens in the light of experience.

The church is an important part of the narrow social community in which Celie is brought up. It is a general meeting place as well as an influence on morals. For instance, she is beaten for supposedly winking at a boy in church. Harpo and Sofia meet there. In the beginning, Celie looks very much to the Church and its idea of God for support, although in practice she gets little help from church-goers. She hopes to manage her difficulties 'with God help', and writes, 'Long as I can spell G-o-d I got somebody along.'

The church, however, turns out to be ungenerous in several ways. Celie cares for it, as she cares for most of those who come into her life, with loving labour. She cleans the floor and windows, makes the wine and washes the altar linen, but is largely disregarded. Very brief approval from the preacher, 'Sister Celie ... You faithful as the day is long,' is all she receives in return – no real acceptance or support. In her turn, Shug is rejected outright, abused and preached against as soon as she appears to be in a weak position. It is true that the preacher 'don't call no name', but equally true that 'he don't have to. Everybody know who he mean.'

As Celie's perception of the world changes, she realizes that the view of God and the Bible which she has grown up with, far from being a help, is actually irrelevant to her needs. For one thing the God of her Church is not of her race. Bitterly, she imagines 'Angels all in white, white hair and white eyes, look like albinos. God all white too, looking like some stout white man work at the bank.' The idea of such a vision offering any kind of deliverance from the pains and difficulties of life is excruciatingly comic. Through Nettie's letters she realizes that she has been misled by a false image created by illustrations white people have added to the text of the Bible, and that the real Jesus had hair 'like lamb's wool', not white racial characteristics at all. Another aspect of her image of God then strikes her: it is male. And she feels just as forsaken by this old grey-bearded man with blue eyes as she does by all the other men in her life.

This revelation comes at a moment of depression, and it is Shug who helps her out of it by providing an alternative image. As the Church rejected Shug, so Shug in turn rejects the narrow Church and its false perceptions, although she in no way rejects religion as an idea. In *The Temple of My Familiar* she founds a Church of her own and is the author of a set of beatitudes known as 'The Gospel According to Shug'. For her, however, 'God ain't a he or a she, but a It'. In order to worship It she can 'lay back and just admire stuff. Be happy'. What she admires is the natural world in its variety of life and love, including sexuality; and her religion is the shared experience of beauty and appreciation of the richness of life. This is the context of the title phrase. God is 'just wanting to share a good thing' so that 'it pisses God off if you walk by the color purple in a field somewhere and don't notice it'. It is this sense of the richness of life which Celie also gradually discovers.

The liberation of Celie comes about when she accepts Shug's view, and the process involves a complete change of attitude. In the beginning she is suspicious of Shug's behaviour and morality. Early on she comments, for instance, on one of Shug's songs, 'Sound low down dirty to me. Like what the preacher tell you it's sin to hear.' But later on, when she has come to accept Shug's values and has asserted her independence and found her confidence, she expresses her new happiness in terms of the two things she has learned from Shug – religion and sexuality: 'Lately I feel like me and God make love just fine.'

Nettie's experience is far removed from Celie's in many ways, but for her, too, the reality she finds in middle age turns out to be different from her early expectations. Going to Africa with Samuel and Corinne as missionaries to 'help the downtrodden people from whom they sprang', the group might be accused of a patronizing attitude at first. But Nettie and Samuel are too honest and too sensitive not to react to the real needs and feelings of the Olinka people, and like Celie they become educated in the variety of forms which religion can take. As soon as they arrive at the Olinka settlement they are confronted by a form of worship strikingly different from their own in the ceremony of the roofleaf, but it is a form which they instinctively respect. The previous missionaries had tried to suppress this form of worship, it seems, 'But the Olinka like it very much. We know a roofleaf is not Jesus Christ, but in its own humble way, is it not God?' This is a point of view which Nettie seems to accept.

Like Shug, she seems at first to feel that the conventions of the Church are restricting. We find, for instance, that she has set aside the pictures supplied by the missionary society and decorated her home instead with native fabrics and mats, which somehow seem more congenial. She absorbs the myths of the Olinka religion, and she writes, 'Even the picture of Christ which generally looks good anywhere looks peculiar here.' What eventually happens is that she arrives at a deeper perception, not limited to narrowly defined images of any kind, but 'more spirit than ever before, and more internal', seeing beyond the forms of worship and seeking for a more personal and direct contact with God. Again, in something of a parallel to Shug, Nettie finds the morality of the Church very narrow. Going to England to seek help for the Olinka people, she discovers that the bishop is much more interested in whether she and Samuel are married or not, an attitude which shocks her in view of the extreme propriety of their actual behaviour towards one another.

As far as the Olinka are concerned, the mission is ultimately a failure. For all the hard work that the missionaries do in teaching and helping, Samuel says, 'The Africans don't even *see* us.' Social and economic conditions eventually force her and Samuel to give up and return to America, but in personal terms Nettie never fails. As with Celie, her love and understanding are constant, and she and her husband return with the idea of founding a new Church in their own country 'that has no idols in it whatsoever'.

Celie's own religion seems eventually to embrace almost all experience. The last letter begins, 'Dear God, Dear stars, dear trees, dear sky, dear peoples. Dear Everything. Dear God.' It is a simple view, and an optimistic one. Religion does not depend on an organized Church, but on shared love, producing a delight in living, of which the richness of the colour purple is a symbol.

The African experience

West Africa is the setting for a considerable part of the novel: all Nettie's experiences as a missionary take place among the Olinka tribe. She approaches the African coast in a state of considerable excitement: 'Something struck in me, in my soul,' she says, 'like a large bell and I just vibrated,' – although this later turns to disillusionment of different kinds.

A primary interest in Africa for the Americans is the connection with their slave ancestors, the discovery of their roots. This, however, turns out to be the first disconcerting element; the Africans themselves do not really want to know about slavery or its effects. They acknowledge no responsibility for it, and actually see the Americans as alien. 'We have seen it all before,' they say. 'You Christians come here, try hard to change us, get sick and go back to England, or wherever you come from.' Samuel, Corinne and Nettie have a certain novelty value because they are black, but the sensation that they are outsiders from a foreign culture is much stronger than any idea of racial unity.

In some ways Nettie is immensely taken with the native culture which she finds in Africa; the hut she has to live in; the appearance of the people; their artefacts. When she considers how their society operates, however, she begins to disapprove. First of all, there is the treatment of women. The Olinka do not approve of the education of women, nor allow them any independence. 'Our women are respected here,' Nettie is told. 'There is always someone to look after the Olinka woman. A father. An uncle. A brother or nephew.' Nettie's own comment is that this reminds her too much of Alphonso; that this 'respect' is in fact subservience. Between her and the Olinka men there is an obvious gap which cannot ever be bridged: they do not approve of her independence, and she can never change their attitudes. Only the one Olinka girl, Tashi, ever comes round to her way of thinking, and she eventually marries Celie's son, Adam, and leaves for America.

Nettie also disapproves of the African customs of female circumcision and of the scarification of young people's faces. The attitude implied here is complex; she understands why these ancient customs still take place in a changing world, that the Olinka are 'carving their identification as a people into their children's faces'. She also sympathizes with the children, scarred against their will and left with painful and often infected wounds as a result. Her position is that of a helpless bystander in a disintegrating society, liking neither its more barbarous customs nor yet the way in which they finally disappear.

The strongest element in the descriptions of Africa is not the impact of the missionaries on pagans, which is for the most part entirely superficial, but the sense of a society in a state of economic turmoil. It is the road driven through their territory which destroys the Olinka, taking away their land for a rubber plantation and smashing their entire culture in the process. Superficially there is progress, with the coast now only a three-day journey away, and the houses roofed with tin instead of leaves. But the Olinka have previously been described as a prosperous and hospitable people. Tragically, they are not aware of the need for resistance until it is too late. They offer the road builders 'goat meat, millet mush, baked yam and cassava, cola nuts and palm wine', only to find their huts flattened by the road without compensation. Their roofleaf, which they regard as holy, is completely destroyed. The destruction of the yam crops accidentally leaves them without protection against tropical diseases. They have become obsolete. It is true that one of the white men who arrives is enthusiastic about learning their language, but only 'before it dies out'.

There is a sense of outrage about what takes place here: the economic exploitation of the land by a foreign company, with no thought for the suffering of the displaced peoples who, after the new distribution of land, are even forced to pay the planters for the water they once owned freely. The only resource of the tribesmen is to run away into the forest from where they can organize 'missions of sabotage against the white plantations'. Ultimately the only thing Nettie and Samuel can do is to leave, to go back to America. There is a sense in which both black Americans and Africans are the victims of white oppression, but very little indication that they can be of much assistance to one another.

Form and style

The idea of writing a novel in the form of letters is not a new one; it goes back almost as far as the history of the novel itself. As early as the mid-eighteenth-century, Richardson's *Pamela* and *Clarissa* both use this form. In some ways it is a natural one to adopt, and it has the advantage of immediacy. The writer is telling us directly about his or her experience soon after it happened.

It does, however, pose certain problems. As with all first person narratives, the viewpoint is limited. It is hard to describe anything of which the narrator does not have personal experience. In *The Color Purple* Alice Walker partly overcomes this by having two narrators, Celie and Nettie, which enables her to widen the range, dealing with some of the themes from different viewpoints. It also enables one of them to supply the other with necessary information which she would otherwise probably not have obtained, for instance the news that Celie's children were not incestuously conceived.

The question of probability remains, however. It is rather a contrived form. Few people in real life write long and detailed letters about their affairs to someone who is sufficiently interested to want minute detail, but far enough away not to be involved personally in the action. There must be an intimacy between the writer of the letters and the recipient, yet a good reason why they cannot meet. Here the sisters are completely separated for thirty years. The reason given why each of them persists in writing letters is the same – loneliness. In each case the writer does not actually expect the letters to reach their destination; they are primarily a means of self-expression. (This is actually so even with Celie's letters to Nettie. She continues to write them after she believes Nettie may be dead.) Celie's early letters are addressed to God as an expression of her complete isolation from friendly human contact. Nettie guesses that Albert has cut her lines of communication with her sister, but continues to write at Christmas and Easter, the family festivals, because she has no other means of reducing her sense of isolation in Africa.

Celie's letters change in style over the series. The first letters are painfully naïve. Her sentences are very short; often only two or three words. Her description of experience, particularly sexual experience, is literal. 'He put his thing up against my hip and sort of wiggle it around,' is the kind of expression that could only come from a child, implying as it does several sorts of ignorance.

The language of Celie's letters is also uneducated. She has been forced to leave school early, so her syntax and spelling are those of black English speech. She uses tenses of the verbs in a different way from standard English: 'she say' where standard English requires 'she says' or 'she said'; 'she be dressed to kill' where standard English is 'she was dressed'. She consistently uses 'us' for 'we' – a point which is specifically noted by Darlene towards the end of the novel. Many of her spellings are a phonetic rendering of her own pronunciation: 'ast' for 'asked', 'teef' for 'teeth', and once, comically, 'two berkulosis'.

This never changes throughout the novel, but her style does become more sophisticated as her experience broadens. The sentence structures become more complex, and the paragraphs longer, though they are often short in comparison with Nettie's. A sense of irony emerges, of which Celie herself is partly conscious. For example, when she tells Shug that she is now writing to Nettie instead of God, Shug objects 'Nettie don't know these people'. Celie's comment is, 'Considering who I been writing to this strike me funny.' Her description of Alphonso's grave as 'something look like a short skyscraper' is deliberately witty.

It is characteristic of Celie's letters right from the beginning that she uses a good deal of direct speech to make her account immediate and dramatic. In the later letters this is often varied by graphic touches of descriptive detail. Sometimes she becomes positively lyrical, for example when she and Shug go to see Alphonso: 'All along the road there's Easter lilies and jonquils and daffodils and all kinds of little early wildflowers. Then us notice all the birds singing they little cans off, all up and down the hedge, that itself is putting out little yellow flowers smell like Virginia creeper.' It is only the humorous 'singing they little cans off' which saves this from sentimentality.

There is a shrewdness and wit in Celie's style which often

emerges in the imagery. The comparisons she makes are drawn from her limited life and domestic experience, but they have a freshness and accuracy of observation. Sofia is described as having 'clear medium brown skin, gleam on it like good furniture', while Mary Agnes is made so presentable 'she smell like a good clean floor'.

The letters from Nettie adopt a totally different style, to distinguish between the two characters. Nettie is the more learned and the more earnest of the two. She is supposed to be the clever one, and she is always anxious to give Celie information, such as 'Did you know there were great cities in Africa, greater than Milledgeville or even Atlanta, thousands of years ago?' or 'The capital of Senegal is Dakar and the people speak their own language.' Her sentences and paragraphs are much longer than Celie's, and her tone rather that of a travel writer, the substance of her writing largely factual, but personalized by frequent questions or exclamations.

Nettie speaks standard English. Although she frequently addresses Celie by name, and uses the occasional incomplete sentence for emphasis, in the main her style is very formal. Take this example, for instance:

> Adam announced his desire to marry Tashi.
> Tashi announced her refusal to be married.
> And then, in that honest, forthright way of hers, she gave her reasons. Paramount among them that, because of the scarification marks on her cheeks, Americans would look down on her as a savage and shun her, and whatever children she and Adam might have.

The vocabulary – 'announced', 'desire', 'paramount', 'scarification' – is formal, the two last being relatively learned and uncommon polysyllables. She uses the conditional 'might', which Celie rarely does. The first two sentences quoted here follow a self-conscious rhetorical pattern, one being a deliberate parallel of the other. The sentence rhythms are measured and complex. Nettie is often enthusiastic, but she usually sounds rather 'schoolmistressy'.

Translated into Celie's dialect this information would read something like, 'Tashi say she not want to marry Adam. She worried peoples look at her and Adam's scars.' The contrast between the two styles is sharp and consistent. A glance at the layout on the page is sufficient to show who is the writer of any given letter, without bothering to examine the salutation. The character of Celie gains much by the contrast, appropriately, as she is the heroine. Nettie's didacticism makes Celie's fresh and lively colloquial speech the more engaging by comparison.

General questions

1 Do you consider this to be an optimistic novel or a pessimistic one?

Suggested notes for essay answer:
First consider the key words of the title. Examination questions have a very precise meaning and you must make sure that you are answering them exactly. Here, whether you decide that the work is optimistic or pessimistic, you must also deal with the evidence on the other side.

Next amass as much material as you can. If this is a coursework essay you can make a list of suitable quotations, with page references, ready for inclusion in your work. In an examination you will not have time, but still make notes of the main points.

Plan a good, logical paragraph structure. Each paragraph should deal with a major aspect of the topic. Save a good point for the end, and avoid merely repeating what you have said before. Illustrate your answer with frequent, brief, and above all relevant quotations.

You might end up with a structure something like this:

> Opening paragraph. Story begins with savage horror. Outrage follows outrage. Celie completely the victim, novel makes important points about the cruelty of society.

> Aspects of cruelty to women, violence, exploitation, no rights or privileges, no help except from one another. African society just as bad.

> Cruelty towards blacks in USA, lynch law, economic exploitation, contemptuous attitudes.

> Vicious treatment of Africa by whites, wanton destruction of tribal society for profit, failure of missionaries.

> This is not the whole story, however. Women help each other. Celie liberated by Shug. Success is possible.

> Society can be changed, individuals capable of understanding, black resilience.

The ending is a happy one, all difficulties resolved. Could possibly be criticized as sentimental, but certainly optimistic. Society possibly not much altered, but final focus entirely on the happy family.

2 In what ways do your reactions to Celie change during the course of the novel?

3 How far is this the story of how Celie learns to fight?

4 Apart from Celie herself, in what other ways do women 'wear the pants' in this novel?

5 Shug Avery is the real heroine of the story. Do you agree?

6 It has been said that the Blues singers were the real feminists of the twenties and thirties. Does your understanding of the character of Shug Avery support this opinion?

7 Are you glad or sorry when Celie refuses to marry Albert for the second time, and why?

8 How do you react to the character of Mr—, and how far is he presented as a monster?

9 What does this novel suggest to us about women's power to determine their own lives?

10 What does the novel have to say about the way black people were treated in the USA in the early twentieth century?

11 'One of the many rapes in the novel is the rape of Africa by colonial interests.' Discuss.

12 How has the novel influenced your view of race relations?

13 What part is played by Millie, Eleanor Jane and Reynolds Stanley in the structure of the novel?

14 Alice Walker sees the Olinka as victims of foreign oppression. Is she, however, wholly approving of tribal society?

15 What parallels exist between Olinka society and that of the USA?

16 What does this novel have to say about family relationships?

17 Organized religion does not seem very helpful to many of the characters in this work. Does that mean that it has a negative view of religion as a whole?

18 To what extent may the success of the novel be attributed to the colloquial style which Alice Walker adopts for Celie's letters?

19 How far do you accept *The Color Purple* as a realistic work?

20 Write one or two letters of your own devising, using *either* Celie's style *or* Nettie's.

Further reading

Other works by Alice Walker

All published in paperback by the Women's Press.

Novels

The Third Life of Grange Copeland (1985)
Meridian (1982)
The Temple of My Familiar (1989)

Stories

In Love and Trouble (1984)
You Can't Keep a Good Woman Down (1982)

Poems

Once (1986)
Revolutionary Petunias (1988)
Good Night, Willie Lee, I'll See You in the Morning (1987)
Horses Make a Landscape Look More Beautiful (1985)

Works on comparable themes

Maya Angelou, *I Know Why the Caged Bird Sings* (Virago, 1984), and subsequent volumes.
Alex Haley, *Roots* (Arrow, 1985)
Ngugi wa Thiong'o, *Petals of Blood* (Heinemann Educational, 1986)